Ethnic Minorities and the Graduate Labour Market

**by John Brennan and Philip McGeevor
with David Alan Gatley and Stephen Molloy**

**A report by the Council for National
Academic Awards for The Commission for
Racial Equality**

ERRATUM
The key in figures 4, 5 & 6 (pp 50-52) is
incorrect. Reverse the
"Matched White Sample" and
"Ethnic Minorities" key.

Published by

Commission for Racial Equality
Elliot House
10–12 Allington Street
London SW1E 5EH

January 1990

© Commission for Racial Equality

ISBN 1-85442-024-0

Price: £2.00

Designed by Chris Bradford
Printed and typeset by Interlink Longraph Ltd

Contents

Contents

Tables and Figures

Tables

Figures

Foreword

In 1988 the Commission published *Employment of Graduates from Ethnic Minorities*, which found disturbing evidence of inequalities one year after graduation for the polytechnic and college graduates of 1982. This research was conducted by the Council for National Academic Awards. The present volume seeks to answer a number of important questions raised by the earlier work. Does the initial disadvantage experienced by ethnic minorities have long-term effects? What is the experience of university graduates compared to that of college and polytechnic graduates? Were the more buoyant labour market conditions of the period after 1982 having different effects for different ethnic groups?

In brief, this report suggests that ethnic minority graduates – like all graduates – do eventually find work, and that, measured in terms of salary levels three years after graduation, the quality of the work is not less favourable. However, it shows too that they have a harder time finding work, that they believe their ethnic origin hinders the search for jobs, that their opportunities for promotion may be more limited and that the work they do is more often not the most preferred. It also shows, ironically, that the success of 'access' policies in the public sector appears to have contributed to ethnic minority students' concentration in certain courses and institutions, with consequential restrictive effects on their career opportunities. A series of interviews with ethnic minority graduates illuminates the personal meanings behind the statistical facts.

For too long, and despite Commission urging, policy makers in higher education and in Government have neglected to take basic steps to determine what is taking place by monitoring the ethnic origins of students. Following the publication of our investigation demonstrating a history of systematic racial discrimination in the admission of medical students, this is no longer the case. From 1990 the clearing houses for both university and polytechnic admissions will be able to provide this information to institutions and to publish general trends. This is most welcome and has great potential benefits for racial equality. Higher education institutions also collect data on graduates' first destinations, and we are hoping that the earliest opportunity will be taken to include ethnic origin in this survey, thereby casting further light on problems faced in the search for work and the nature of a careers counselling and guidance service sensitive to ethnic minority students' needs. Better information will also help employers actively seeking to implement equal opportunity policies to assess and target their recruitment methods.

The Commission's experience shows that equality of opportunity demands the steady application of informed and targeted policies. Many employers of graduates now accept this principle, and the Association of Graduate Recruiters has given it expression in support for the steering committee on racial equality in which it combines with the Association of Graduate Careers Advisory Services. We hope this report and the new data which will be available in the 1990s will help the associations and their members to mark the decade as the time when equality in opportunities for ethnic minority graduates was definitively established.

Michael Day
Chairman

Acknowledgements

Under Section 43 of the Race Relations Act 1976 the Commission has a general duty to work towards the elimination of racial discrimination and to promote equality of opportunity and good relations between persons of different racial groups. The Commission can undertake research itself, or finance research that is undertaken by others. It was in this context that we funded this research project.

This report was produced for the Commission by the Council for National Academic Awards (CNAA). We are grateful to John Brennan and Philip McGeevor for this. Several other people contributed to the work, in particular David Gatley, Stephen Molloy, Elizabeth Lebas, and Kate Murray. The officers from the CRE who assisted with the report were Joe Charlesworth (Employment Division), Shaista Faruqui, Lata McWatt and Cathie Lloyd (Research Section).

Dr Muhammad Anwar
Principal, Research Section

Chapter 1

Introduction

In 1987 the Commission for Racial Equality (CRE) published our report on *Employment of Graduates from Ethnic Minorities.* It contained the results of a survey of 2700 graduates from polytechnics and colleges, some six per cent of whom were from ethnic minorities, mainly Asian. It focused on the experiences of graduates in the first year after leaving college. It found that the ethnic minority graduates – who, like the rest of the sample, had graduated in the summer of 1982 – experienced more difficulties than white graduates in making the transition from higher education into the labour market. They were more likely to be unemployed, and the qualification and salary levels of the jobs they did obtain tended to be lower. The graduates themselves perceived greater difficulties in obtaining employment than did their white counterparts.

However, the report left a number of important questions unanswered; chiefly, whether those initial disadvantages had longer-term effects. Many of the graduates in the 1982 sample – white as well as ethnic minority had not even entered the labour market when we first contacted them in the summer of 1983, either through initial unemployment or because they had remained in full-time education. In addition, our other work on graduate employment had indicated that early destinations were not always a reliable guide to later ones (Brennan and McGeevor 1988). Consequently, we felt that it would be important to see what happened to the ethnic minority graduates in the period following that initial transitional year.

A second unanswered question concerned the universities. The 1982 sample of graduates had been drawn exclusively from polytechnics and colleges. There is evidence to suggest that university graduates fare rather better in the labour market than their polytechnic and college counterparts. What then of ethnic minority graduates from universities?

The employment prospects for new graduates in 1982 were particularly poor. Employer demand for graduates has steadily improved since then, and a shortfall is predicted in the 1990s. Thus, a further question concerned the employment experiences of graduates in more buoyant labour market conditions. Consequently, we felt that it would be useful to look at the experiences of a more recent cohort of graduates, and this time to include graduates from universities.

A rather different set of questions required explanations. These centred around what Troyna and Jenkins (1983) have referred to as the 'stubborn fact' that educational qualifications do not appear to give ethnic minority people the same advantages in employment as they give to whites. Qualifications are an advantage in the labour market, but they are less of an advantage to Britain's ethnic minority population. Does this hold true for graduates, and if so, what are the processes within the educational system and labour markets that are responsible? How does ethnic background interact with other characteristics to limit opportunity? To attempt to answer these sorts of questions, we moved away from survey evidence to talk to some of the graduates personally as well as to some of the people responsible for their education.

The CRE provided funding to enable us to undertake a further programme of work consisting of four main elements:

1. analysis of information collected from the original 1982 sample over the *three* years following their graduation;
2. a second survey of graduates from colleges, polytechnics and universities, the sample selected from the cohort of graduates in 1984 and contacted in the summer of 1987;
3. a series of interviews with graduates from the original 1982 sample; and
4. a series of interviews with staff of higher education institutions – in particular, careers advisors.

This report uses this programme of work to consider further the employment prospects of Britain's ethnic minority graduates, the factors that influence them and the actions that may lead to their improvement. Where other evidence exists, we have used it, sometimes at length, to support conclusions and inferences that could only be drawn tentatively, if at all, from the work directly commissioned by the CRE.

In the next chapter, we describe the six main sources of research evidence on which this report is based. In chapter three we examine key features of the educational experience of ethnic minorities in Britain, features which we believe are crucial to an understanding of subsequent labour market experiences. Graduate employment is not just a matter between employers and graduates; it concerns crucially the opportunities available to young people within the education system and the factors – economic, historical and organisational – which influence them. These are reviewed in chapter three, drawing both on published materials and on the experiences of the ethnic minority graduates from our own surveys.

In chapter four we present the major findings on the employment experiences of ethnic minority graduates in Britain. We examine problems of entry into the labour market, generally short-lived if painful at the time, and the quality and character of the jobs eventually obtained. We consider both objective factors – types of jobs and salary levels – and how the graduates interpret and respond to their experiences.

In chapter five we consider some evidence of a rather different sort. We consider the views of careers advisors and others within higher education institutions who work with ethnic minority students and have seen at first hand the kinds of problems they face.

Our report is based on evidence provided by the graduates themselves, augmented by the perceptions of careers officers and others. The major omission is the views and perspectives of employers and recruiters of graduates. Although we make some reference to studies that have included employer perspectives, they have not been the major focus of our own study. Nevertheless, many of the conclusions and recommendations which we draw in chapter six concern employers directly, and, we hope, will prompt responses and commentaries from employers in other forums.

Chapter 2

Research Undertaken

In addition to the work funded by the CRE, this report draws on data derived from two other major surveys of graduates. The data sources were as follows:

1. A follow-up survey of CNAA graduates from 1982, contacted in 1983, 1984 and 1985.
2. A special survey of CNAA and university graduates from 1984, contacted in 1987, funded by the CRE.
3. A follow-up survey of CNAA and university graduates and BTEC diplomates from 1985, contacted in 1987.
4. A Government survey of graduates and diplomates from 1980, contacted in 1986.
5. Interviews with a sample of ethnic minority graduates, undertaken in 1987.
6. Interviews with staff from higher education institutions, undertaken in 1987 and 1988.

The survey of 1982 CNAA graduates

The survey of 1982 graduates undertaken by the CNAA as part of its Higher Education and the Labour Market research programme (HELM 82) was a longitudinal study of approximately ten per cent of the 1982 cohort of the graduates from CNAA full-time and sandwich degrees. Graduates received questionnaires in the summers of 1983, 1984 and 1985. The survey consisted of a sample of 122 courses from 33 polytechnics and colleges chosen on the basis of geographical spread and institutional type. An attempt was made to contact all graduates (excluding overseas graduates) from these courses. The sample was selected in order to explore relationships and therefore did not purport to be a representative random sample of CNAA graduates. Nevertheless, the sample was broadly reflective of the numbers graduating in the main faculty areas as represented by the CNAA subject committee structure as it existed at the time of the start of the project in 1983. The courses were selected as being representative of the range of courses found within these faculty areas. Only one major area of CNAA course provision was excluded completely; this was teacher education.

Our earlier report for the CRE was based on this sample using data collected one year after graduation. This report uses more recent data collected two and three years after graduation. A major problem was the decline in the response rate of the ethnic minorities over the three years of the project.

Table 1 shows that whereas 6.4 per cent of the sample were African, Afro-Caribbean and Asian at the time of first contact in 1983, these groups comprised only 3.3 per cent of the sample at the third point of contact in 1985. The ethnic minority graduates were more likely than other graduates to live in London and this may partly account for the greater difficulty in re-contacting them. When first contacted, 47 per cent lived in London compared with only ten per cent of the white UK graduates. Ethnic minority graduates who had been living in London were less likely to reply to the third questionnaire than ethnic minority graduates living in other places. By 1985 London graduates comprised only 32 per cent of the sample of ethnic minority graduates while the proportion of white graduates living in London actually rose from ten per cent to just under 14 per cent. This suggests that location and the housing arrangements of new graduates may affect the response rate. However, it remains, at best, only a partial explanation. Whatever the reasons for it, it limits the conclusions that can be drawn from this particular sample.

Table 1   Response rates, by ethnic origin (1982 sample)

	1983		1984		1985	
	No.	%	No.	%	No.	%
African	22	.9	9	.5	4	.3
Afro-Caribbean	19	.8	6	.4	7	.5
Asian	120	4.7	51	3.1	33	2.5
UK European	2282	90.2	1549	94.1	1266	94.5
Other	86	3.4	31	1.9	30	2.2
Total	**2529**	**100**	**1646**	**100**	**1340**	**100**

The CNAA/CRE survey of 1984 graduates

The sample was selected in such a way as to attempt to maximise the numbers of graduates from ethnic minorities. This was done by targeting courses and institutions that, on the evidence of the earlier 1982 survey, were expected to contain a relatively high proportion of ethnic minority graduates. The courses were business studies, electrical engineering and pharmacy (for Asian graduates), and humanities, law and social science (for Afro-Caribbean graduates). Sixteen polytechnics and seven universities were contacted, with an emphasis on institutions in areas known to have large ethnic minority populations. The names (but not the addresses) of polytechnic graduates were available from the CNAA and this enabled a sample to be drawn from the specified courses at the institutions. No names were available from the universities, and an attempt was therefore made to contact all graduates from the specified courses. Letters to graduates were addressed and forwarded to the institutions. The letters explained the purpose of the survey and asked the graduates if they were prepared to take part. A pre-paid postcard was enclosed on which graduates who agreed to participate were asked to write their names and addresses. When the postcards were returned, the graduates were posted a copy of the questionnaire together with a postpaid envelope. This process was completed by April 1987. Because of the lack of addresses it was generally not possible to send out reminders or prompts to non-respondents. This was the main cause of the relatively low response rate of 40 per cent to the survey of 1984 graduates.

The proportion of ethnic minority students on each course is shown in Table 2. Whereas the method of sample selection worked reasonably well in locating ethnic minority graduates in the polytechnics, it failed to do so in the universities.

The survey of 1985 graduates

In 1985, the CNAA commissioned a further survey of graduates, this time including control groups of university graduates and holders of higher diploma awards of the Business and Technical Education Council (BTEC).

Twenty-four subject areas were chosen to reflect a wide range of course types, both vocational and non-vocational. The selection of

Table 2 Course of Study, by ethnic origin (1984 sample)

	African No.	Caribbean No.	Asian No.	Afro-Asian No.	Total ethnic minority No.	%	Total on course No.
CNAA							
Humanities	3	1	1	—	5	6.2	80
Electrical Engineering	2	3	8	3	16	20.0	80
Law	2	3	7	3	15	19.2	78
Pharmacy	2	1	18	6	27	21.4	126
Social Science	1	7	—	—	8	8.8	91
Business Studies	—	2	7	2	11	10.2	107
Total	10	17	41	14	82	14.6	562
University							
Pharmacy	—	—	—	—	0	0	67
English/History	—	—	—	—	0	0	50
Social Science	—	1	—	—	1	4.0	25
Electrical Engineering	—	—	3	1	4	3.7	108
Total	—	1	3	1	5	2.0	250
Total CNAA and University	**10**	**18**	**44**	**15**	**87**	**10.7**	**812**

courses was made with the further aim of ensuring some comparability with the 1982 cohort. Names, but not addresses, of the CNAA graduates in the sample were obtained from the CNAA and a random sample of 150 male and female graduates was selected from each subject area. In most cases the polytechnics and colleges forwarded the letters and questionnaires to the graduates. In the case of the university and BTEC samples we had neither the names nor the addresses. As a result, we selected a sample of courses and attempted to contact all of the graduates from those courses via their institutions. The overall response rates were 53.4 per cent for CNAA graduates, 51.1 per cent for university graduates and 47.8 per cent for BTEC diplomates. The ethnic profiles of the resulting

Table 3   Ethnic minority graduates in the four survey samples

	1980[1]		1982[2]		1984[3]		1985[4]		All surveys	
	No.	%	No.	%	No.	%	No.	%	No.	%
African	13	.1	22	.9	10	1.2	12	.3	57	.4
Caribbean	27	.3	19	.8	18	2.2	20	.6	84	.5
S. Asian	73	.8			44	5.4	58	1.6	175	1.3
East African Asian	34	.4	120	4.8	15	1.9	20	.6	69	.5
{ (combined)									364	2.3
All ethnic minority	147	1.6	160	6.4	87	10.7	110	3.0	504	3.2
Other	441	4.9	86	3.4	46	5.7	233	6.4	806	5.1
White UK	8346	93.4	2280	90.2	679	83.6	3298	90.6	14603	91.8
All graduates	8934	100.0	2527	100.0	812	100.0	3641	100.0	15914	100.0

Notes

1. A ten per cent sample of all higher education qualifiers. (Includes qualification below degree level). University and public sector higher education.

2. A sample of courses in 33 subject areas. All CNAA degrees.

3. Sample targeted at courses and institutions with high proportion of ethnic minority graduates. University and public sector higher education.

4. Random sample of male and female graduates from 24 subject areas in university and public sector.

samples are given in Table 3, which gives similar information for each of the four samples included in this study.

The Government survey of 1980 graduates

The national survey of 1980 graduates and diplomates was commissioned by the Department of Employment and the Department of Education and Science. The survey was carried out by Social and Community Planning Research (Field and Meadows 1987). The population eligible for inclusion in the sample was defined as follows: (i) started or completed a course as full-time (including sandwich) student; (ii) domiciled in the United Kingdom; (iii) obtained a first degree or diploma or similar qualification involving at least two years' full-time study post 'A' level. Excluded from the survey were overseas students, part-time students and those who failed to obtain a qualification in 1980.

All universities, polytechnics and colleges in England, Wales and Scotland which had more than 40 students in the 1980 cohort were included. Of the 198 eligible institutions 169 cooperated in the survey. One in six university students and one in four polytechnic and college students were selected giving a total target sample of 18 575. The achieved sample was 8948, that is 49 per cent of the target group. However, if those graduates who were known definitely not to have been reached (no known address; returned by Post Offices, etc) are excluded, the response rate was 65 per cent. Only one per cent actually refused to participate. Full details of the sample are available in the methodological report (Field and Meadows 1987).

The questionnaire was piloted on the 1981 graduates from one university, one polytechnic and one college. A controlled experiment was incorporated in the pilot to test whether response varied according to the inclusion of a question on ethnic origins. No difference in response rate was found.

Interviews with graduates

A total of 18 interviews with ethnic minority graduates were conducted in order to provide more qualitative information about their experiences in education and employment. Thirteen had graduated in 1982; and five in 1984. Five were Afro-Caribbeans (four females and one male); one was from West Africa (female); four were East African Asians (three males and one female); one was Sri Lankan (male); six were from India (four females and two males) and one was from Pakistan (male). With the exception of the man from Sri Lanka all were UK citizens and had received at least part of their secondary education in Britain.

While no claims can be made for the representativeness of this sample, each account of the individual's experiences and perceptions is valid in its own right and can illustrate and give insight into the processes that underpin the broad trends indicated by the survey.

Interviews with staff from higher education institutions

Twenty-one interviews were carried out. Five of these were with careers advisors in polytechnics, four in London, one in the East Midlands. Three were interviews with careers advisors at universities in the London area. One was with a polytechnic assistant director who had responsibility for equal opportunities at the polytechnic and two were with teaching staff responsible for sandwich placements. The remaining ten interviews were conducted with members of staff at a northern college of higher education. Although the latter is one of the largest post-school institutions in the country, it offers the relatively low number of six degree courses, with an annual intake of about 300 students. Interviews were conducted with the vice principal responsible for higher education, the senior careers advisor, the heads of the departments of Teaching Studies and Vocational Placement, three placement tutors and three course directors.

Note on methodology

In order to attempt to identify the independent effects of ethnic background a matched sample was selected on the basis of course taken, sex, degree class and institution attended. The technique was simply to list these variables together with the ethnic background of all the cases and then, for each person of African, Caribbean or

Asian background to attempt to select a matching white British person. In the majority of cases an exact match was possible, and in all cases a match for course and sex of graduate was made. Where an exact match could not be made the same type of course, degree class and sex was sought at another institution. In a few cases where no match was possible on degree class the nearest degree class was chosen on an alternating lower then higher basis – thus randomising any effect of degree class. This process, therefore, eliminated any differences between ethnic minority and white graduates resulting from course of study, gender or degree class. This procedure was carried out for the 1982, 1984 and 1985 samples. Reference in the text, Tables and Figures to 'matched sample' is to groups so selected.

Other factors which influenced the employment of the graduates in these samples have been discussed extensively elsewhere (Brennan and McGeevor 1988), and the effect of social class has been the subject of a separate report (Gatley 1988). The impact of social class and other background characteristics is complex, but in no cases were differences found that would account for the effects of ethnicity described in this report.

Throughout this report we have used the term 'Asian' to refer to graduates who, on a self-completion questionnaire to 1982 graduates, designated themselves as 'Asian/UK Asian', or, on the questionnaire to 1984 and 1985 graduates, indicated that they were of 'Bangladeshi origin', 'Indian origin' or 'Pakistani origin'. Similarly, we have used the term 'East African Asian' for those who indicated this in the 1984 and 1985 surveys. We have used the term 'Caribbean' for those responding in 1982 as 'Caribbean/UK Caribbean' or in 1984 and 1985 as being of 'Caribbean origin'. We have used the term 'African' for those responding in 1982 as 'African/UK African' or in 1984 and 1985 as being of 'African origin'. In some Tables where numbers of individuals in particular ethnic groups were too small for analysis, we have aggregated African and Caribbean respondents into an 'Afro-Caribbean' category. We have used the words ethnic minority in the text as a general term to identify British graduates from all these backgrounds.

Chapter 3

Educational Experiences of Ethnic Minorities in Britain

In this chapter we look briefly at the demographic characteristics of British ethnic minorities and at some of the evidence of their educational achievement and participation in higher education. We go on to consider the characteristics of the graduates in our own surveys in the light of this evidence.

Background

Members of ethnic minorities are mainly to be found in urban areas. *Social Trends* (Great Britain Central Statistical Office 1988, p 26) shows that while 31 per cent of the white British population are resident in metropolitan areas, the corresponding figures for the British population of West Indian, Bangladeshi, and Indian and Pakistani origin are 81 per cent, 79 per cent and 66 per cent respectively. Similarly the 1984 Labour Force Survey estimates that 58 per cent of British workers of West Indian or Guyanese ethnic origin are resident in Greater London – compared to only 11 per cent of white workers (Barber 1985, p 471). This distribution has implications for the kind of schooling available to the majority of ethnic minority children.

The ethnic minority community is younger than the rest of the population. Thus, 70 per cent of the Bangladeshi, 68 per cent of the Pakistani and 59 per cent of the Indian and West Indian populations are under 30 years of age compared with 42 per cent of the white British population (*Social Trends* 1988, p 26). As the young tend to be better qualified, and are more likely to be in non-manual employment, great care must be taken in interpreting figures of overall level of qualification and socio-economic status.

There are differences in the types of work done by different ethnic groups. Ethnic minority men are overrepresented in 'distribution, hotels, catering and repairs', and 'transport and communication'. They are underrepresented in 'construction', 'agriculture', 'energy' and 'extraction' as well as 'services' (except health).

Ethnic minority women are less likely to be in 'education', 'banking and financial services' and more likely to be in 'health service' or 'other manufacturing' (*Employment Gazette* 1987, p 22).

It would appear that an ethnic minority person is less likely to be in a non-manual occupation. Brown found that 15 per cent of West Indian men, 26 per cent of Asian men and 42 per cent of white men were in non-manual work (Brown 1984, p 305); the proportions for women were: 62 per cent of white women in non-manual work compared with 53 per cent of West Indian and 48 per cent of Asian women. Brown also notes large differences within sectors in terms of level of job. White men in manufacturing industry were four times as likely as West Indian men and more than three times as likely as Asian men to be in non-manual jobs (Brown 1984, p 305). A much higher proportion of ethnic minority people were in non-manual work in the public sector than in the private sector (Brown 1984, p 306).

The type and level of their work made ethnic minorities more vulnerable to the economic recession in the early 1980s. The growth in unemployment among ethnic minority people between 1974 and 1982 is one of the major trends referred to by Brown (the other being the growth in self-employment among people of Asian origin).

Unemployment is particularly acute for ethnic minority workers. The 1987 Labour Force Survey showed a relationship between ethnic background and unemployment: ethnic minority unemployment stood at 16.4 per cent compared to 10.2 per cent for whites. (There were variations between different ethnic minority groups, with West Indian/Guyanese, Indian and Pakistani/Bangladeshi groups having unemployment rates of 17 per cent, 13 per cent and 29 per cent respectively (*Employment Gazette* 1988, p 153).) While unemployment is much less for those with educational qualifications, the proportional difference between ethnic minority and white men is greater. Thus the 1985 Labour Force Survey showed that for those with higher qualifications, three per cent of whites and ten per cent of ethnic minorities were unemployed (that is, over three times as many). For those with other qualifications, it was nine per cent for whites and 21 per cent for ethnic minorities (over twice as many). For those with no qualification, it was 17 per cent for whites and 26 per cent for ethnic minorities (1.5 times as many) (*Employment Gazette* 1987, p 27). To put it another way, for a white male gaining a higher qualification reduces the likelihood of unemployment five and a half times; for an ethnic minority male it reduces it only two and a half times.

Unemployment for ethnic minority women is roughly double that for white women: 19 per cent compared to 10 per cent. However, there is no difference among those with higher qualifications. At six per cent, the proportion of women with higher qualifications who are unemployed is more than white men but less than for similarly qualified ethnic minority men. Among women with other qualifications the rates of unemployment for whites and ethnic minorities are ten per cent and 32 per cent, for those with no qualifications they are 12 per cent and 20 per cent.

These statistics all indicate that although the attainment of educational qualifications improves the employment prospects of ethnic minority graduates, the improvement is nothing like as great as it should be.

The Swann report (1985) examined the level of achievement of ethnic minority pupils in British schools. It concluded that racism played a part in under-achievement, but it appeared far more equivocal than the early provisional report (Rampton 1981), except in the more limited case of West Indian children, where the evidence was clear-cut. The reason for the reticence was the apparent success of Asian students in spite of racism and discrimination. As a result, the causes of educational achievement were seen to 'lie deep within their respective cultures' (Swann 1985). The evidence cited by Swann for the educational success of Asian students is open to question (Tanna 1985). The fact that 'Asian children stay on longer at school than other children and achieve slightly below the national average in overall levels of academic achievement' (Swann, p 116) is open to various interpretations. Would anybody consider it a sign of employment success to work longer hours for slightly less money?

A majority of studies which have compared Asian and white educational achievement have suggested under-achievement by Asian children (Tomlinson 1980). In any assessment of the evidence two factors need to be borne in mind. First, because of the patterns of residence of ethnic minorities the schools attended are less likely to be geared to admission to higher education. Second, the use of parents' occupation as a measure of social class may be inaccurate when applied to ethnic minorities. Because of earlier discrimination, many highly qualified ethnic minority people were unable to get jobs commensurate with their skills. Allan, Bentley and Bonnet (1972) found that many ethnic minority graduates could only find manual work following migration to the UK. Similarly, the studies by the Policy Studies Institute show that a significant proportion of educated ethnic minority people are in manual employment (Smith 1977 and Brown 1984). Thus, it is probably the case that, for some ethnic minorities at least, families will possess considerably more 'cultural capital' than white families in a similar economic position.

The ethnic background of applicants to higher education has not until now been recorded by the bodies responsible for admissions to universities and polytechnics. Decisions have now been made to collect this information in the future. Such information will not only provide firm evidence on the participation of ethnic minorities in higher education but will also allow scrutiny of the admissions procedure. Work by McManus and Richards (1984) suggested that candidates with non-European surnames were less likely to be admitted to a London medical school. Collier and Burke (1986) found that different London medical schools had remarkably consistent ratios of European to non-European students over a three year period – suggesting the possibility that a quota system was being operated.

The absence of ethnic monitoring makes an accurate assessment of ethnic minority participation in higher education difficult. Vellins (1982) looked at the numbers of South Asian and East African born, but home fee paying, students entering universities in 1979. Besides showing a concentration in particular disciplines, particularly medicine and pure science, her work clearly demonstrates the different participation rates of various south Asian groups. Thus for UK born men 11.6 per cent went to university: the figures for East African, Indian, Pakistani and Bangladeshi born students were 15.5 per cent, 12.2 per cent, 7.0 per cent and 1.8 per cent respectively. Similarly, 7.6 per cent of UK born women went to university, compared with 8 per cent of East African, 4.2 per cent of Indian, 1.7 per cent of Pakistani and 1.6 per cent of Bangladeshi born women. Thus participation was very low for Pakistani women and Bangladeshi men and women (Ballard and Vellins 1985).

Craft and Craft (1983) analysed results from 16 outer London secondary schools with high proportions of ethnic minority pupils (nine per cent West Indian, 24 per cent Asian and 13 per cent 'other'). They found that while class had an important role in determining participation in the sixth form for West Indian and white pupils it had little effect on Asian pupils. Seventy-eight per cent of working class Asians wished to enter the sixth form compared to 52 per cent of West Indian and 38 per cent of white pupils. Other relevant findings were that West Indian pupils were

25

more likely to go to further education colleges than to stay on in the sixth form, and that Asian sixth formers were less likely than whites to go to university. While 51 per cent of whites did so, only 19 per cent of Asians gained entry to university. This is partly explained by the number of Asians using the sixth form to gain further 'O' levels, but even if only those sixth formers doing two or more 'A' levels are considered, 57 per cent of whites compared with 42 per cent of Asians went on to university.

The value that ethnic minority communities place on education is well documented (Gupta 1977, Kitwood and Borrell 1980). The value of education in improving employment prospects is also recognised (Brooks and Singh 1978 and Verma 1985). The result is a higher proportion of young people from ethnic minority groups staying in education beyond the minimum school leaving age. The 1985 Labour Force Survey shows that 13 per cent of white males between the ages of 16 and 24 were students – compared to 16 per cent West Indian, 36 per cent Indian, and 42 per cent Pakistani/ Bangladeshi. The corresponding figures for women are 12 per cent (white), 14 per cent (West Indian), 27 per cent (Indian), and 13 per cent (Pakistani/Bangladeshi).

To summarise the existing evidence on the educational experiences of ethnic minorities, we can say that:

1. Ethnic minority pupils are more likely to have parents who are in manual work (or unemployed).
2. Ethnic minorities are likely to live in areas and attend schools that have a poor academic record and that do not have a tradition of entrance into higher education.
3. Ethnic minority parents place great value on education and, in the case of South Asians, this seems to transcend traditional class barriers; working class Asians appear to aspire to higher education to the same extent as their middle class peers.
4. The route to higher education for many ethnic minority people is via further education rather than sixth forms.
5. Ethnic minority students are likely to be older than white students at the time of entry to higher education.

The evidence of the surveys

We now turn to the results of the recent graduate surveys. In the context of the overall experiences of ethnic minorities in the education system described above, the graduates on whose experiences this report is based constitute the system's successes. As we shall see, in most cases against considerable odds, they have made significant educational achievements. Not only have they gained entry to university, polytechnic and college degree courses, they have successfully completed them – they are graduates.

The influence of home

The home can provide the knowledge, support and encouragement that assists a successful educational career. The educational experiences of parents are likely to affect both their ability and willingness to assist in their children's education. Ethnic minority parents appear to value highly their children's education, and our interviews with graduates provided examples of this.

My father came over to this country to study law and then did his barrister's exams – as a mature student – when I was ten years old. [Asian female]

My parents wanted to send me to college, especially my dad. He came to this country to give us all a good education, which I don't think he could have achieved back in India. He always admired the education in England. Education is always valuable no matter what. Over the years we have not made a lot of money – he's OK financially, but in education and learning he is much richer. He is richer than anyone I know in this respect. [Indian female]

More typical was active support and encouragement, but without knowledge based on experience:

When I was younger I got into grammar school and my mum always encouraged me to do my best. She always took an interest in my school, obviously not my work because she was uneducated, but she always encouraged me to do my best. It was a matter of taking one hurdle at a time. [Afro-Caribbean male]

At the other extreme were parents with no experience of higher education and for whom their children's educational ambitions seemed unusual and possibly eccentric. For example, two of the Afro-Caribbean women were in this position:

I didn't have any encouragement from my family because my family were obviously ignorant about it; if they knew it they would have told me, but they didn't know. [Afro-Caribbean female]

Evidence from the surveys shows that ethnic minority graduates are more likely than their white counterparts to come from a home where parents are in manual occupations (although, as mentioned earlier, this may itself be the result of earlier discrimination). As Table 4 shows, barely one in ten Caribbean graduates had a white collar background. A similar distribution is indicated for the graduates in our 1984 sample. That survey used slightly different categories (Afro-Asian and not East African Asian), but the overall message is the same.

Table 4   Parents' socio-economic group, by ethnic origin (1980 and 1984 samples)

Socio-economic group*	Asian %	East African Asian† %	Caribbean %	African %	White UK %
1980 sample					
Professional	11.0	11.8	—	38.5	16.9
Employer/Manager	6.8	5.9	—	7.7	23.5
Intermediate	15.1	26.5	11.1	30.8	19.7
Skilled manual	38.4	26.5	11.1	7.7	23.0
Semi-skilled	11.0	17.6	29.6	—	5.0
Unskilled manual	5.5	—	14.8	7.7	1.0
Not classified	12.3	11.8	33.3	7.7	10.9
	(73)	(34)	(27)	(13)	(8346)
1984 sample					
Senior managerial	2.8	7.1	—	25	13.1
Senior professional	11.1	7.1	—	25	23.5
Other prof/manag	5.6	—	15.4	—	17.8
Intermediate	44.4	50	15.4	50	25.7
Manual	36.1	35.7	69.2	—	20.3
	(36)§	(14)§	(13)§	(8)§	(596)§

* Mother's or father's socio-economic group, whichever is higher.
† The category used in the 1984 was slightly different – Afro Asian.
§ Eight Asian cases, one East African Asian case, five Caribbean cases, two African cases and 83 White UK cases were missing in the 1984 sample.

Note Figures in brackets are numbers in the sample.

The influence of school

Table 5 shows that ethnic minority graduates are more likely than whites to have received a comprehensive secondary schooling. However, the culture of comprehensive schools can vary considerably, and, as was noted in the previous section, the pattern of settlement means that many Afro-Caribbean and Asian pupils may attend schools that lack strong traditions of entry to higher education. One result of this may be the greater importance of colleges of further education as a route to a degree course for ethnic minority students.

Table 5   Type of school, by ethnic origin (1980 and 1984 samples)

Type of School	Asian %	East African Asian* %	Caribbean %	African %	White UK %
1980 sample					
Comprehensive	38.4	32.4	51.9	15.4	35.4
Grammar/direct grant	23.3	14.7	22.2	23.1	37.2
Secondary Modern	19.2	8.8	11.1	7.7	5.7
Sixth Form College	1.4	2.9	—	—	4.8
Independent	2.7	5.9	—	23.1	11.5
Further Education College	12.3	26.5	11.1	—	3.5
Abroad	1.4	2.9	3.7	23.1	.3
Other	1.4	5.9	—	7.7	1.6
	(73)	(34)	(27)	(13)	(8346)
1984 sample					
Comprehensive	61.9	60	50	10	44.4
Fee-paying	7.1	6.7	—	30	13.4
Grammar	7.1	6.7	22.2	40	31.8
Secondary Modern	16.7	13.3	27.8	10	7.9
Other	7.1	13.3	—	10	2.5
	(42)†	(15)	(18)	(10)	(673)†

* The category used in the 1984 survey was slightly different – Afro Asian.
† Two Asian cases and seven white British cases are missing.

Note Figures in brackets are numbers in the sample.

Table 6   Entry qualifications, by ethnic origin (1984 sample)

	Asian %	Afro Asian %	Caribbean %	African %	UK European %	Other %	All %
Non standard	7.0	—	22.2	20.0	9.4	10.9	9.6
Standard	79.1	86.7	55.6	30.0	78.4	71.7	77.1
Technical	14.0	13.3	16.7	20.0	9.6	8.7	10.1
Other	—	—	5.6	30.0	2.5	8.7	3.1
	(43)†	(15)	(18)	(10)	(668)†	(46)	(800)

† One Asian case and 12 UK European cases are missing.
Note Figures in brackets are numbers in the sample.

Moving on to a consideration of entry qualifications, Table 6 shows the 'highest' qualification obtained by graduates at entry to higher education. Taking two or more GCE 'A' level passes as standard entry it can be seen that 77.1 per cent of *all* graduates fell into this category, 10.1 per cent had technical qualifications (HNCs, BTECs, etc), 9.6 per cent were non-standard entrants (with less than two GCE 'A' level passes) and 3.1 per cent had other qualifications. African and Caribbean graduates were the least likely to have had standard entry qualifications and the most likely to have been non-standard entrants.

The interviews suggested that some pupils succeed in spite of, rather than because of, the school they attended. The school experience may limit a student's chances of achieving higher education: through negative stereotyping by the teaching staff, the hostility of other pupils, or simply by not being a very good school and thus lessening the opportunity for all its pupils, white or ethnic minority. There was a variation in the extent to which these different factors were mentioned by the graduates we interviewed. Negative attitudes of staff were more likely to be referred to by the Afro-Caribbeans in our sample; and the hostility of other pupils, by the Asians. Poor schooling was mentioned by both groups.

> *At school I found it affected me because . . . I'm not saying the teachers were racialist but they had this narrow-minded view that if you were black or West Indian all you had to do was do sports or anything practical in that sense rather than concentrating on you academically.* [Afro-Caribbean female]

When I went to school, it was a grammar school; a lot of the kids that went there came from middle class backgrounds . . . I came from a pretty poor family. We didn't . . . you know there was only me mum and she wasn't very well so I would get things like free school dinners and that kind of thing. You did get kids from affluent families. There were 90 of us in the first year's intake and only four of us were black. So . . . I did get some kind of prejudice. I remember the headmaster, he used to do the racist stereotype things a bit. There were four of us and he used to call me by someone else's name. I'm pretty sure he knew I wasn't that person . . . it was another black guy. He used to deliberately do it to try and wind you up a bit. It was only the headmaster . . . most of the teachers were great. [Afro-Caribbean male]

Several comments suggested that students had attended schools where negative attitudes of teachers had the effect of depressing the horizons and aspirations of all students in the school:

I was told if I wanted to be a nurse what I had to do, that's all they went on about, nursing or working in a bank as a clerk. They didn't go on to the higher professions, not lawyers or doctors or accountants or anything like that. Things like that were sort of unheard of in the school we went to. It was always typing . . . why don't you do typing? [Afro-Caribbean female]

Some teachers underestimate the sort of students they've got, so when you go for a reference or something like that they don't say 'alright then, let's hope you get that place', they say 'come off it', phrases like 'I don't think you can get those sort of grades' rather than 'put some effort into it'. They have a negative attitude. [Indian male]

Problems of discipline in the school were contrasted with earlier schooling. Among the East African Asians in particular there was a view that their schooling in Africa had been of a higher standard and that that had conferred particular advantages on them in the transition to English schools:

The first thing that struck me here was the unruly behaviour of the kids in school. I couldn't believe it. Our maths lesson and English lesson were very easily disrupted. You got jeered if you did well – the wrong attitude to school. It wasn't only from the coloured people, it was the whole school. [East African Asian male]

Unruly behaviour in school could be linked to discrimination by pupils:

> *There was some discrimination from some of the students at 'O' level – spitting at you, that sort of thing, but there wasn't any at 'A' level.* [East African Asian male]

Three of the graduates had attended grammar school and this would seem to have increased the likelihood of entrance to higher education. For those students who did not go to a selective secondary school there appears to have been two ways forward. First, the progress of a few able pupils might be sponsored by the commitment of some of the teachers. Thus, one Asian woman said:

> *A few teachers who were very supportive seemed to have particular interests . . . out of a number of us that went into the sixth form there was only seven of us that were actually doing three 'A' levels – a lot were retaking 'O' levels or doing one or two; so of the seven we got a lot of specific attention from some of the teachers to push us to do well and go on further.* [Asian female]

Second, in some cases there appears to have been a subculture of students within the school who were committed to going on to higher education. Here, a group of motivated students would decide that higher education was the way forward for them. Three of the Asian male graduates referred to such a supportive subculture:

> *We had five or six friends together and we said, 'Oh how about sticking together and going to higher education', and we said 'Yes, that's a good idea'. So that's how it basically started, and once we were in that we just liked it and stayed there and that was the way we got into higher education.*

(Were they all members of your community?)

> *Yes, at the moment one is a pharmacist, one is a chemist and one is a computer scientist, and I just went into engineering.* [Indian male]

Type of higher education institution

The ethnic minority graduates in our studies had in many cases overcome severe obstacles to gain entry into higher education. However, higher education is not homogeneous, certainly not as far as employment prospects are concerned. The value of a degree in the labour market depends crucially on the subject or subjects studied and, to only a slightly lesser extent, on the type of institution attended. Despite the large scale growth and recognition of the non-university sector of higher education, it remains the case that a polytechnic or college place is a second choice for many students. There is also evidence to suggest that many employers regard them as second choice as well and prefer to recruit their graduate personnel from the universities.

The polytechnics and colleges of higher education have, however, placed increasing emphasis in recent years on extending access to higher education groups that have traditionally been under-represented. These policies on extending access have frequently been focused on people in the institutions' local communities. Given the primarily urban location of most of the English polytechnics, this has often meant a substantial ethnic minority community.

The evidence from the representative 1980 survey is that ethnic minority students are less likely to attend university than white British students. Whereas almost 55 per cent of white students were to be found in the universities, only the Asian students came anywhere near this proportion with 47.9 per cent. The importance of polytechnics in providing higher education opportunities for ethnic minorities is emphasised by the figures in Table 7. It is also worth noting that in this large 1980 sample, ethnic minority graduates formed only 1.6 per cent of the total.

The figures derived from the most recent surveys we conducted ourselves are not directly comparable. Of those which included the universities, only the 1984 survey did so on an equal footing with the polytechnics and colleges, and then only in a limited number of subject areas. Nevertheless, the failure of this survey to identify significant numbers of ethnic minorities at all is further evidence of their underrepresentation in the university sector. The results of the introduction of more systematic ethnic monitoring are therefore to be awaited with considerable interest, not just for the light they will shed on sector differences but for the possibilities which they will provide for identifying distinctive institutional and subject profiles.

As we have already noted, the type of institution attended may crucially affect a person's career chances. Studies of graduate employers have suggested preferences for graduates from universities (Roizen and Jepson, 1986). This was suspected and resented by the ethnic minority graduates from polytechnics who valued their own educational experience highly. One graduate said:

There is more discrimination between place of education than

Table 7   Type of higher education institution, by ethnic origin (1980 and 1985 samples)

	Asian %	East African Asian %	Caribbean %	African %	White British %	Other %	All graduates %	No.
1980 sample								
University	47.9	38.2	29.6	20.8	54.9	56.9	54.7	(4889)
Polytechnic	42.5	58.8	40.7	38.5	27.0	25.6	27.2	(2431)
Other colleges	9.6	2.9	29.6	30.8	18.2	17.4	18.1	(1614)
	(73)	(34)	(27)	(13)	(8346)	(441)	(8934)	(8934)
1985 sample								
University	8.6	20.0	5.0	91.7	22.9	26.2	22.6	(812)
Polytechnic	84.5	75.0	95.0	8.3	61.5	61.7	62.2	(2235)
Other colleges	6.9	5.0	—	—	15.7	12.1	15.3	(546)
	(58)	(20)	(20)	(12)	(3334)	(149)	(3593)*	(3593)*

* Forty-eight cases were missing.
Note Figures in brackets are numbers

*colour of skin. I'm sure an Indian who studied at a polytechnic
and got a first would not get a job which an Indian with a first
from a university went for. There is more discrimination between
polytechnic and university.* [Indian male]

The same graduate felt that promotion aspects could also be
affected.

*It really annoys me because at the place I'm working there are lots
of graduates, a few women, and their degree is no better than
mine – in some cases it is, in some cases it is not – but because they
are the typical graduates and have been to university rather than
to poly they have risen above me and I get really frustrated.*
[Afro-Caribbean female]

A majority of graduates had applied to university and had failed
to achieve high enough grades at 'A' level to gain entrance.
Exceptions were: the graduate who did not apply for university
because he did not have 'O' level English; and another, who was
offered a place at a university subject to obtaining an industrial
sponsor – which he could not get. There was one person whose 'A'
levels were probably sufficient, but who did not apply because of
family commitments; those commitments almost prevented him
from entering higher education at all.

*It was really my family background; my parents were divorced
and my mum wasn't working and there was my younger brother.
I didn't really want to put a lot of pressure on my mother. So I
thought I would get a job and take it from there. That was my
main thinking behind it* [joining a bank straight from school].
*But then I spoke to my mum about it and she encouraged me and
said we would manage. I stayed at home so we would manage on
the grant. So I thought I'd see how it goes, if I got further
qualification that could only be a help in the future . . . When you
are at college you are dependent on your parents to some extent.*
[Afro Caribbean male]

The attractions of the 'local' polytechnic were also mentioned by
other graduates:

*I chose _____ for the silliest reason really. It was near to
where I live . . . it was near to my parents. I didn't want to leave
home at the time and the course seemed suitable. Also my best
friend was going there . . . someone I knew. The course itself just
seemed normal. To tell you the truth I couldn't really distinguish*

at that stage whether I was going for the best type of legal course I could go for in a polytechnic or wherever, it was a challenge anyway just to go there. [Afro-Caribbean female]

I did get accepted in X Poly. I decided to go to Y Poly. With X I was a bit worried that I wouldn't be able to get along with the people. I thought the people would be sort of high-powered . . . especially students, and because it sounded so posh, and I thought how am I going to communicate with people like that? Whereas in Y it's local and I thought I would be able to get along with people better. [Afro-Caribbean female]

The last two responses illustrate several themes: the desire to stay near home, lack of information about the reputation of particular courses and a fear that some institutions of higher education may be alien and threatening. The attractions of studying near to home were also mentioned by a number of the Asian men:

It was easy to commute to from my place . . . being sort of family-oriented I preferred to go within London. [Indian male]

I had three or four polys that made me an offer and out of these I said I would stay at home – if I could get the same degree without travelling miles away – that was a big factor. [Indian male]

Two Asian women mentioned the desire to get away from home as a reason for their choice of course. In one case this was regretted:

I decided to go to _____ poly in the first place because I had decided to get away from home and get away from London. I thought it would be quite nice to have that sort of campus. But then I think I found that I didn't relate very well with the other people on the course and also I found it very isolated down there as well, so after the first year, before the end, I decided I'd move back to London and do the course here . . . I think part of that was that it wasn't cosmopolitan and that was the reason I felt so isolated . . . I was really pleased I moved back to London. I just felt really in tune with the people around me and I was happy with the course content. [Indian female]

The cosmopolitan atmosphere of the London polytechnics in particular was referred to and valued by the graduates. In some cases, as illustrated by the next quotation, it was valued because of the shared background of some of the students. However, a more typical response was to value the cultural mix of the institution.

*The ethnic people dominated the polytechnic. If you go to a
university it is the other way round. It was beneficial. You felt
within your own community.* [Indian male]

*Being in halls, you are a little community within a bigger one.
You're not all of the same background or on the same course.
There were 18 of us sharing that kitchen. We became our own
little crowd. We had everyone there in our kitchen. We had an
Iranian, someone from Singapore, someone from Ethiopia, a
smattering of natives from all over the country – we even had a
major's son – we had quite a good mixture.* [East African Asian
male]

Choice of higher education institutions is influenced by all sorts of
factors. For many students, choice is severely limited by attainment
at secondary school, and the 'second best' of a polytechnic or
college place becomes the only option. However, for several of the
students we interviewed a polytechnic place had been the limit of
their aspirations. The graduates expressed much loyalty to their
polytechnics, particularly where strong multicultural institutions
had been created. For some students, the opportunity to live at
home while studying had also been an important consideration.
These graduates would have resented any suggestion of 'second
best' about their polytechnic education, but some of them did feel
that their job prospects suffered by comparison with their university
counterparts.

Type of subjects studied
The small number of students from ethnic minorities in higher
education makes it difficult to reach any authoritative assessment of
patterns of subject choice. Our interviews with academic staff
suggested that local circumstances could cause considerable variation between higher education institutions, reflecting the subject
mix of the institution and the catchment area of its recruitment.

What is clear is that ethnic minorities are not evenly distributed
across all types of courses. Thus, engineering courses have a
relatively high proportion of ethnic minority students, the overwhelming majority of whom are Asian males. In some polytechnics
and colleges, particularly those located in the inner cities, there are
large numbers of ethnic minority students on social science courses,
but in this case the students are more likely to be Afro-Caribbean,
female, older and working class. Some major subject fields (in terms
of student enrolments) appear to recruit virtually no students from

ethnic minorities; arts and humanities courses appear to be in this position. However, we would not be surprised to find individual institutions which confounded these trends.

The kind of subject studied within higher education is important for two reasons: first, employment prospects for graduates differ substantially according to subject; and second, the same processes that lead to subject concentrations may also lead to employment concentrations.

Of the four sets of survey data at our disposal, the 1980 and 1985 samples were the most representative of the total student body and, as such, provided the most useful guide to the overall subject distribution of ethnic minority graduates. Table 8 shows the most popular subject groups for ethnic minorities in the 1980 survey.

Table 8 Subject distribution of ethnic minority graduates (1980 sample)

	All graduates No.	All Ethnic minority graduates No.	%	Ethnic minority graduates as % of subject group %
Education	855	7	4.8	.8
Medicine, Dentistry and Health	206	11	7.5	5.3
Engineering & Technology	1242	31	21.1	2.5
Agriculture, Forestry and Veterinary	155	0	—	—
Biology & Physical Science	1682	36	24.5	2.1
Administrative, Business & Social Studies	2269	41	27.9	1.8
Architecture & other Professional Vocational Studies	370	1	.7	.3
Languages, Literature & Area Studies	888	3	2.0	.3
Arts and other languages	882	6	4.1	.7
No answer	385	11	7.5	2.9
All subjects	**8934**	**147**	**100**	**1.6**

Within these broad groupings there are concentrations of particular ethnic groups in specific subjects. Thus, 3.6 per cent of the whole 1980 sample did electrical engineering, but 9.6 per cent of Asians, 8.8 per cent of East African Asians and 14.8 per cent of Caribbeans took the subject. Pharmacy was taken by all of 0.8 per cent of the whole sample, but by 17.6 per cent of East African Asians and a further 4.1 per cent of Asians. Indeed, these two groupings provided 12.9 per cent of all pharmacists. Sociology and combined social science accounted for 5.5 per cent of the total sample, but 18.5 per cent of Caribbean graduates.

Table 9 shows the distribution of graduates from the 1985 survey. Among CNAA graduates there were similar clusters: overall, 3.6 per cent of the CNAA graduates were from ethnic minority backgrounds; the proportions were greatest in law (11.3%), science (10.1%), social science (10.0%) and computing (8.9%). Three courses had no ethnic minority graduates in the sample: fine art (78 graduates), quantity surveying (100 graduates) and urban estate management (142 graduates). The latter two courses were characterised by excellent job prospects.

The 1985 university sample of graduates was based on a sample of courses from a limited number of institutions and thus subject to possible bias. Even with these reservations there appear to be far

Table 9   Subject distribution of ethnic minority graduates (1985 sample)

	All graduates No.	All ethnic minority graduates No.	%	Ethnic minority graduates as % of subject group %
Arts & Humanities	487	4	3.7	.8
Art & Design	376	5	4.6	1.3
Social Science	1021	46	42.6	4.5
Science	503	30	27.8	6.0
Engineering	380	12	11.1	3.2
Other	737	11	10.2	1.5
All subjects	**3504**	**108**	**100**	**3.1**

fewer ethnic minority graduates than one would expect; less than one per cent overall (seven out of 711). In all surveys which included university students the proportions of ethnic minority students were much smaller than in the comparable polytechnic and college samples.

Figures 1 and 2 summarise the subject distributions of the 1980 and 1985 samples, contrasting the distribution of ethnic minority students with other students in the samples.

The benefits of higher education

In our previous report we were able to conclude that, despite difficulties encountered in the graduate labour market, ethnic minority graduates' perceptions were that the benefits they had received from higher education were substantial. In general they rated the benefits more highly than did white graduates. The evidence provided by the subsequent surveys, while supporting the general picture, is less clear-cut.

All graduates, irrespective of ethnic origin, institution attended or subject studied, tended to respond positively to questions about the benefits they had received from higher education. As far as general educational benefits were concerned, the differences between the ethnic groups in our samples were not substantial. Benefits such as improved abilities in critical thinking, organising work and applying knowledge were perceived by about 70 per cent of all graduates in our samples. Similar proportions felt that they were more self-confident and independent as a result of their higher education. The major area of difference between the ethnic minority graduates and their white counterparts concerned a sense of responsibility: increasing the individual's sense of responsibility was a much more important benefit of higher education for ethnic minority graduates than it was for whites. Tables 10 and 11 summarise the benefits perceived by the graduates in the 1984 sample, using samples of ethnic minority and white graduates matched for subject of study, gender, institution and age.

A slightly different picture emerged when we asked specifically about career-related benefits. Again, the benefits were regarded as substantial, but, in some important respects, less so for ethnic minority graduates. Tables 12 and 13 summarise the results for the Asian and Afro-Caribbean graduates from the 1984 sample.

The survey evidence was supported by the graduate interviews. When asked if their higher education had been worthwhile, those

**Figure 1 Subject distribution of ethnic minority graduates
(1980 sample)**

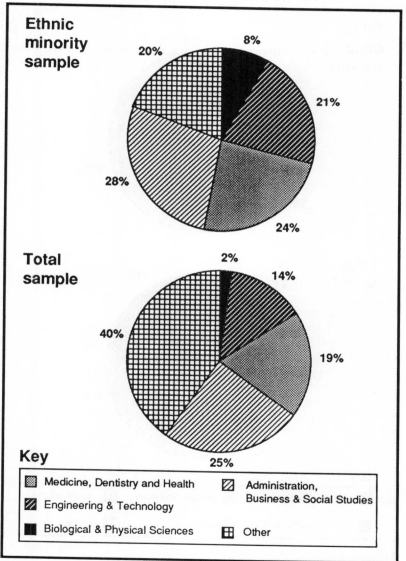

Ethnic minority sample

20%
8%
21%
24%
28%

Total sample

2%
14%
19%
40%
25%

Key

Medicine, Dentistry and Health

Engineering & Technology

Biological & Physical Sciences

Administration,
Business & Social Studies

Other

**Figure 2   Subject distribution of ethnic minority graduates
(1985 sample)**

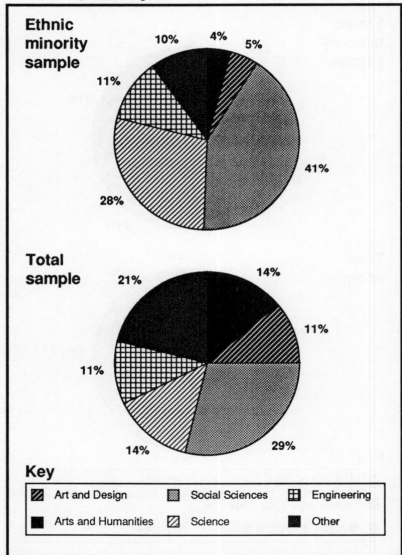

Table 10   Abilities and attributes improved by higher education: Afro-Caribbeans (1984 sample)

	Afro-Caribbean %	Matched %	Difference %
Abilities			
Spoken communication	60	58	2
Written communication	66	64	2
Cooperating with people	52	50	2
Critical thinking	86	77	9
Organising my work	72	65	7
Leadership	40	26	14
Application of knowledge	73	78	−5
Use of numerical data	55	37	18*
Logical thinking	69	61	8
Attributes			
Sense of responsibility	56	39	17*
Self confidence	78	62	14**
Political awareness	52	36	16
Understanding other people	60	57	3
Independence	68	65	3

* Significant at ten per cent level.
** Significant at five per cent level.

interviewed were unanimous in saying that it had, even when it had not led to the career they were hoping for. Their responses tended to stress the benefits in terms of personal development rather than vocational application.

It probably made me more of an extrovert than an introvert. I used to be quite shy. It gave me confidence. [East African Asian male]

It was worth it because I enjoyed myself. I learned something and I learned skills that I can use, so yes, I think it was worth doing. [Indian female]

When you are 18 you're very immature, to be honest, and you have to become more independent, because when you are at school everything is done for you. At college you are given much more independence and they treat you like an adult. You have to learn how to sort out your work and your different projects and essays. So it's a kind of period when you've got other people around you but you have the chance to be more independent. It increases your education plus your insight into other things. It broadens your horizons. [Afro-Caribbean female]

It did change me. You get more confidence. When I was 18 I was a bit more kind of reserved. It gives you more self-confidence. It hasn't given me the job I would dearly like, but obviously having a degree is still useful. [Afro-Caribbean male]

I'm much more confident in myself than what I was before I did it. I realised that I'm capable of doing something, I have achieved something which makes me think, well, you know there is something in me, whereas at school, you have made a fool of yourself in your fifth year, you just doubt yourself and what you can do. It's given me strength and character, it really has. [Afro-Caribbean female]

Table 11   Abilities and attributes improved by higher education: Asian (1984) sample)

	Asian %	Matched %	Difference %
Abilities			
Spoken communication	52	55	−3
Written communication	55	54	1
Cooperating with people	62	58	4
Critical thinking	67	71	−4
Organising my work	67	73	−6
Leadership	46	36	10
Application of knowledge	66	68	−2
Use of numerical data	49	53	−4
Logical thinking	65	68	−3
Attributes			
Sense of responsibility	68	56	12**
Self confidence	74	71	3
Political awareness	35	28	7
Understanding other people	66	55	11*
Independence	74	78	−4

* Significant at ten per cent level.
** Significant at five per cent level.

Table 12 Benefits of higher education: Afro-Caribbeans (1984 sample)

	Afro-Caribbean %	Matched %	Difference %
Career aims			
Getting an interesting job	59	65	−6
Securing a good income	46	59	−13
Made it easier to get a job	56	70	−14
Improved long term job prospects	63	78	−15
Increased early earnings	38	56	−18
Enhanced long term earnings	57	61	−4
Improved quality of work	68	63	−5
Other			
Improved social status	46	38	8
Becoming a widely educated person	56	54	2
Having time to sort out ideas	39	44	5
Learning about a chosen subject	72	69	3

Table 13 Benefits of higher education: Asians (1984) sample)

	Asians %	Matched %	Difference %
Career aims			
Getting an interesting job	71	84	−13*
Securing a good income	68	70	−2
Made it easier to get a job	80	87	−7
Improved long term job prospects	79	90	−11**
Increased early earnings	62	65	−3
Enhanced long term earnings	71	80	−9
Improved quality of work	66	74	−8
Other			
Improved social status	61	51	10
Becoming a widely educated person	61	54	7
Having time to sort out ideas	42	38	4
Learning about a chosen subject	62	74	−12**

* Significant at ten per cent level.
** Significant at five per cent level.

   In this chapter, we have looked at the social and educational backgrounds and experiences of ethnic minority students up to the point of graduation. The students in our samples represent the high achievers of the ethnic minority communities. In the next chapter we consider how far high educational achievement provides the basis for achievements in the labour market.

Chapter 4

Employment of Ethnic Minority Graduates

The transition from higher education to work

Higher education both increases a person's chances of well paid employment and decreases the likelihood of unemployment. The 1987 Labour Force Survey showed that the level of unemployment for people with a degree or equivalent was 4.1 per cent; for people without qualifications it was 15.1 per cent (*Employment Gazette* 1988, p 153). However, this survey also showed a relationship between ethnic background and unemployment: ethnic minority unemployment stood at 16.4 per cent compared with 10.2 per cent for whites.

It seems unlikely that the discrimination and disadvantage that ethnic minorities face at other levels in the job market disappear with the acquisition of a degree. As has been shown, highly qualified men from ethnic minorities are more than three times as likely to be unemployed as similarly qualified white men (*Employment Gazette* 1987, p 27). Eggleston (1986) shows that at each level of qualification ethnic minority respondents in his survey were more likely to be unemployed. Smith (1977) found that racial discrimination was highest for clerical, management trainee and accountancy jobs. Dex (1982) saw that a qualification held by ethnic minority persons seemed to have less exchange value than the same qualification held by a white person, and Jenkins (1986) concludes pessimistically:

There is thus no likelihood that parity in the market for educational qualifications or training will bring equality of opportunity in the labour market.

Ballard and Holden (1975) examined the labour market experiences of 60 ethnic minority graduates. They found that ethnic minority graduates were more likely than their white peers to continue in full-time education and that a motive for this was their anticipation of labour market difficulties. Ethnic minority graduates made more applications, but gained fewer interviews. The different experiences of ethnic minority and white graduates could not be explained by sex, social class or degree results.

In our previous report we noted the greater difficulties that ethnic minority graduates had encountered in entering the labour market and the significantly higher levels of unemployment that existed among them one year after graduation. As with other graduates, early unemployment does not continue long. As Figure 3 indicates, three years after graduation most of the 1982 sample of graduates, irrespective of ethnic origin, were employed. A similar picture was found with the 1984 sample. See Table 14.

Figure 3   The transition to employment (1982 graduates)

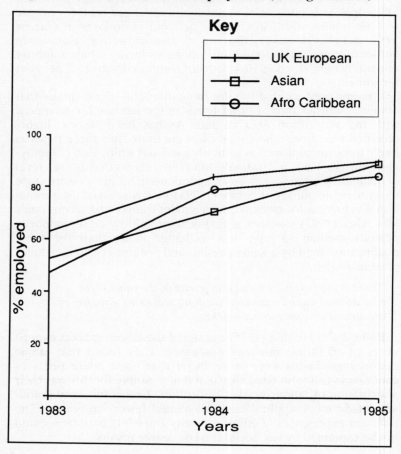

Table 14 Destinations of 1984 graduates three years after graduation, by ethnic origin

	Asian No.	Afro Asian No.	Caribbean No.	African No.	UK European No.	Other No.	All No.
Employed	37	14	17	6	606	41	721
Full-time study	5	0	0	2	32	3	42
Unemployed	1	0	0	2	14	1	18
Other	1	1	1	0	23	1	27
Total	44	15	18	10	675*	46	808

* Four cases were missing.

Figures 4, 5 and 6 show the month-by-month percentages in full-time employment, full-time study and unemployment for the matched samples of 1985 graduates. As can be seen ethnic minority graduates were more likely to be in full-time study and less likely to be in full-time work. Unemployment in the first few months after graduation is much more common for non-white graduates. It is 17 per cent higher in the September after graduation, 16 per cent higher in October and 13 per cent higher in November.

An examination of the sectors of the economy in which the graduates from 1984 were employed three years after graduation shows distinct differences between the ethnic groups. See Table 15. It shows that 31.5 per cent of the sample were employed in the public sector, 23.1 per cent in manufacturing, 35.7 per cent in commerce and 9.8 per cent were self-employed. Afro-Asians and, to a slightly lesser extent Asians, were by far the most likely to be self-employed, and Caribbean and African graduates were the most likely to be employed within the public sector. Relatively few African and Caribbean graduates were employed in manufacturing and commerce, and Afro-Asian graduates were the least likely to be employed in the public sector.

The distinctiveness of the sector distribution of ethnic minority graduates comes out most clearly when we compare them with UK European graduates matched according to subject studied and gender. Combining the 1984 and 1985 samples, Table 16 shows the distribution of ethnic minority graduates and their matched sample according to the three broad employer types, which excludes the

**Figure 4   Graduates in employment, month-by-month from
September 1985 to May 1987 (1985 sample)**

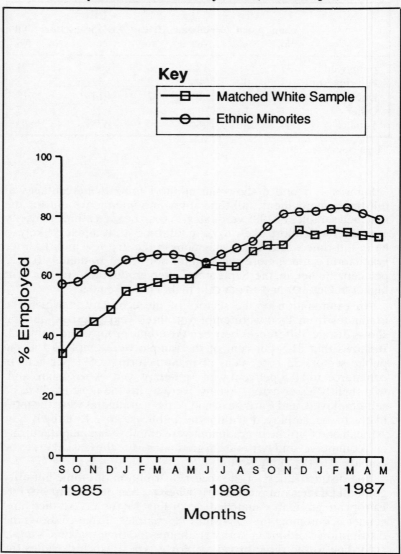

Figure 5   Graduates in full-time education, month-by- month from September 1985 to May 1987 (1985 sample)

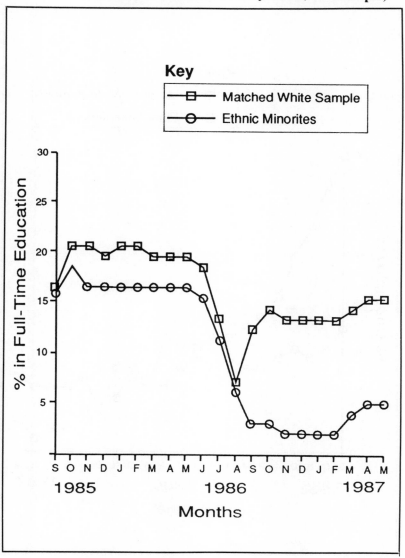

Figure 6   Unemployed graduates, month-by-month from September 1985 to May 1987 (1985 sample)

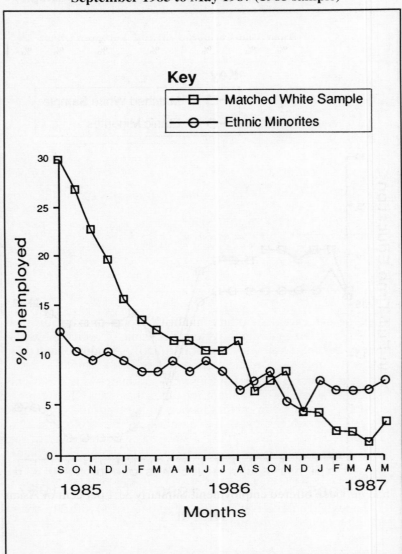

Table 15   Sectors of employment, by ethnic origin (1984 sample)

	Asian %	Afro Asian %	Caribbean %	African %	UK European %	Other %	All %
Public sector	25.6	13.3	52.9	66.7	31.7	23.1	31.5
Manufacturing	17.9	20.0	5.9	16.7	23.6	30.8	23.1
Commerce	30.8	33.3	23.5	16.7	36.5	38.5	35.7
Self-employed	25.6	33.3	17.6	—	8.3	7.7	9.8
	(39)	(15)	(17)	(6)	(606)	(39)	(722)

Note Figures in brackets are numbers

self-employed. Overall, ethnic minority graduates are significantly more likely to be employed by the public and voluntary sectors. This is true for each of the ethnic minority groups considered. Graduates from Caribbean or African backgrounds also seem less likely to be employed by manufacturing and allied industries.

Applying for jobs

There is evidence that ethnic minority groups make more job applications, but get fewer job offers. See Table 17, which shows the number of applications made by ethnic minority graduates and their matched sample in their final year at college (1984 sample).

The implication is that ethnic minority graduates were experiencing greater difficulty in obtaining job offers than their UK European equivalents. Some support for this view comes from an examination of Table 18 which shows the number of job offers made to graduates: both Asian and Afro-Caribbean graduates were less likely to have been offered a job during their final year in higher education. Overall, of those applying, 57.9 per cent of Afro-Caribbean, but only 38.5 per cent of their matched counterparts, had *not* been offered employment. Similarly 35.1 per cent of Asian graduates had not received any job offers compared with 20 per cent of their matched counterparts.

The 1985 survey produced similar results (see Table 19). The finding that 72.2 per cent of ethnic minority graduates did not

Table 16   Type of employer (1984 and 1985 samples combined)

	Asian %	Matched %	East African Asian %	Matched %	Caribbean %	Matched %	African %	Matched %	All ethnic minorities %	All Matched %
Public/voluntary	33	26	32	15	58	36	60	38	40	27
Manufacturing	29	28	24	22	8	32	10	31	22	28
Commerce	38	46	44	63	35	32	30	31	38	45
	(66)	(76)	(25)	(27)	(26)	(22)	(10)	(16)	(127)	(141)

Note Figures in brackets are numbers.

Table 17   Job applications during final year at college, by ethnic origin (1984 sample)

No. of job applications	Afro Caribbean %	Matched %	Asian %	Matched %
1–2	21.0	53.8	16.2	33.3
3–4	15.8	15.4	13.5	20.0
5–9	21.0	7.7	16.2	22.2
Over 10	42.1	23.1	54.1	24.4
	(19)	(13)	(37)	(45)

Note Figures in brackets are numbers.

Table 18   Job offers during final year at college, by ethnic origin (1984 sample)

	Afro-Caribbean %	Matched %	Asian %	Matched %
None	57.9	38.5	35.1	20.0
One	31.6	53.8	32.4	35.6
Two	5.3	7.7	21.6	26.7
Three +	5.3	—	10.8	17.8
	(19)	(13)	(37)	(45)

Note Figures in brackets are numbers

receive job offers in their final year (compared with 52.6 per cent of the matched sample) helps explain the earlier finding that ethnic minority graduates were more likely to be unemployed in the first few months after graduation.

A study of the recruitment of examiners in the insolvency service (Tavistock Institute 1978) found that 19 per cent of white candidates were offered a place compared with five per cent of ethnic minority candidates. The ethnic minority candidates were more likely to have had higher education and a degree than the white candidates.

This pattern of a lower success rate at each stage of the job hunting process was also found by the CRE in its examination of chartered accountancy training contracts (CRE 1987) and by Tanna (1987). Her study of South Asian university graduates showed them

Table 19   Job offers during final year at college and since graduation (1985 sample)

	Ethnic minority %	Matched %
Final Year		
None	72.2	52.6
One	13.4	25.8
Two	9.3	13.4
Three	3.1	1.0
Four +	2.1	7.2
Since graduation		
None	32.0	22.7
One	17.5	32.0
Two	21.6	18.6
Three	12.4	10.3
Four +	16.5	16.5
	(97)	(97)

Note Figures in brackets are numbers.

to be better qualified, more willing to accept a lower starting salary, and to have started searching for work earlier. They made more applications, and more reached the first, second and third interview stages. However, they were less likely to be offered a job at each stage.

We asked the graduates directly how difficult it had been to find suitable employment. Table 20 shows clearly that both ethnic minority groups had found it more difficult to find suitable employment than their matched samples. Overall, 52 per cent of Asian graduates said they had little difficulty in finding suitable work – a high figure which reflects the relatively favourable subjects studied. Their matched counterparts had even less difficulty, with almost 76 per cent claiming a relatively untroubled entrance to the labour market. Virtually twice as many Asians reported that it had been very difficult getting a suitable job. The Afro-Caribbean sample also found greater difficulty than their matched sample. Only 20 per cent reported little difficulty and 36 per cent said it had been very difficult.

Table 20   Experience of finding employment, by ethnic origin (1984 sample)

	Afro-Caribbean %	Matched %	Asian %	Matched %
Very difficult to get any job	36.0	22.7	21.7	11.1
Difficulty in finding the right job	44.0	50.0	26.1	13.3
Little difficulty	20.0	27.3	52.1	75.6
	(27)	(22)	(46)	(45)

Note Figures in brackets are numbers.

The experience of applying for jobs and being rejected is almost always unpleasant. It is often accompanied by a lowering of expectations. Certainly this response was common to several of the graduates we interviewed.

After I left college I had a period of unemployment for about a year. During that time I applied for quite a lot of jobs. I can't remember exactly how many a week, but it feels like I was filling out applications every week. By the end of that year of unemployment I was prepared to do any job. Ideas about career development or whatever had gone out of the window. [Indian female]

I was on the dole until early November. Before the exams I had made about ten or 15 applications and after the exams about 30 or 40. _____ were the only company that offered me a job. After the applications I only had four or five interviews. . . . I wanted to go into communications. The kind of job I wanted I didn't get. [Indian male]

For example when I finished my finals . . . one would think that after getting your finals one would get articles easily . . . but it wasn't as easy as I thought . . . so I expect a similar sort of situation when I finish being in articles. I hope it won't be the same, but I am expecting the worst. It's the best way to be, then I won't get disappointed. It was really depressing last time actually.

57

[Afro-Caribbean female]

Faced with these difficulties graduates made the best of it, but the outcome of these hard choices was to confirm the skewed distribution of ethnic minorities in employment.

(**Q** Is your career developing as you expected?)
No. When I left college back in 1982 I didn't really go out with the idea of joining the local council. I've been with the council for two and a half years and I have progressed as I thought I would. But it was a matter of accident. What I really wanted to do was to go and work for one of the stores, like Marks and Spencer, and be a management trainee, because I had done a marketing course and I thought that would be interesting. But really, the opportunities were not there when I left college. I did go to Woolworths for an interview; they wanted 25 trainees and had over 500 applicants. The competition was very fierce for jobs like that. [Afro-Caribbean male]

In the next example, someone who had wanted a career in pharmacological research (having done an applied biology degree) became a sub-postmaster.

I had one interview in that whole period. Letters? numbers? I must have reached 100 at least. I have a folder that thick up there. I was resigned to the fact that I wasn't getting anywhere with the job applications, so working with my parents was the next best thing – and as it turns out I like the job I am doing now. [East African Asian male]

Graduates typically expressed a suspicion that their ethnic background might be playing a part in their employment difficulties; but if there was racial discrimination, then it was largely invisible.

When I was working at the pharmacy and we had a locum working there, he was one of these old chaps who had seen the world and knew everything about it, and he came up to me one day after enquiring about my job applications and said, 'Have you ever thought that the only reason you are not getting a job is because you're black?' I said, 'I've never looked at it like that. If it is, I'm not going to know.' He said, 'Could it be that they just look at your name, know you are foreign and just don't want to know?' I said, 'If that is the case I'm never going to find out, because all I get is a letter'. [East African Asian male]

One graduate felt more confident in asserting that discrimination had taken place, because he had a reference point in the experiences of other graduates on his course.

After I graduated I think prejudice was involved in that. On the course, of the British students there were four English students and five Asians, and before the exam results had even come out they were all offered jobs, and of all the Asian students – who were all British citizens – none had offers. And after the results came out you could see who – of the two groups – was the better group. Statistically you should have gone for the Indians if you were going on the grades alone. I would say at that point it was prejudice that was holding us back. [Indian male]

This graduate is assuming that academic ability should be the most important criterion in the recruitment of graduates. However, several studies of employers have demonstrated the importance attached to personal characteristics when recruiting new employees (Roizen and Jepson 1985 and Gordon 1984).

What are these qualities that employers of graduates are looking for? Gordon found that a majority of recruiters thought that graduates were more productive than non-graduates doing similar work, and saw them as being flexible, ambitious and highly motivated. They valued the knowledge base of pure and applied science graduates and the communication skills of arts and social science graduates. However, in many cases the criteria of job worthiness move away from what Jenkins (1986) calls 'suitability' (skills directly related to the capacity to perform a job) towards 'acceptability' (abilities only indirectly related to the job, such as personality, ability to fit in, etc). Notions of acceptability use criteria which are difficult to assess. As Jenkins says:

The notion of acceptability, particularly when it interacts with ethnic stereotypes, is likely to be systematically detrimental to black workers.

In other words, an ethnic minority graduate may be suitable for a job in the sense of having the skill and capacity to perform the job, but he or she may be less acceptable because inferences are drawn about personality and ability to fit in on the basis of ethnic background.

It has been argued that many employers have an idealised stereotype of the sort of person they are looking for rather than a set of criteria appropriate to a specific job. Thus, the graduate should be young and have pursued extra curricular activities, should be bright but not too studious, and should be a good mixer (with other similar people). One might also add that graduate interviewers are often inexperienced (Keenan 1978) and frequently favour interviewees who are similar to themselves (Rand and Wexley 1975).

It is these imprecise conceptions of 'acceptability' that can be crucial in a job interview. First impressions are significantly more important than the rest of the interview (Blakeney and McNoughton 1971). Springbelt (1958) suggested that minds were made up in the first four minutes and that opinion movements thereafter were more likely to move from positive to negative. That is to say that while you can still 'foul up' an interview it is very difficult to redeem an initial poor impression.

Our interviews with graduates revealed situations where the first impression appeared to have been one of shock and surprise.

I remember going for an interview with _____ bank once when I was younger, and he asked me questions like how long have you been in this country. Now on the application form it said I was born in this country . . . you still get that. You go for certain jobs and on the application form I put that I was born in Birmingham, so a couple of times I've been to jobs where you get an initial look of surprise on their face because you are black.
[Afro-Caribbbean male]

The names of most Asian students should have made the interviewer's look of surprise unlikely. However, one Asian graduate spoke of an unpleasant interview experience – presumably by an interviewer whose own communication skills were deficient.

When the _____ interviewed me on the milkround I did feel that the interviewer was [prejudiced] – in fact the other Asian students felt it. As soon as they came out of the room they said, forget it you're not going to get the job. I didn't. I felt in the way he approached me, I felt he was prejudiced and I knew then that he wasn't going to offer me the job. I did feel that this man . . . well his approach wasn't very good at all. [Indian male]

Levels of jobs

One important indicator of the level of a job is income. It has the big advantage of being an objective indicator, but there are difficulties with it, principally that of the effect of geography. As was shown earlier, ethnic minority graduates are more likely to be living in the London area, and the measure of income includes London allowances in the total. The second difficulty is the extent of missing data. Figures 7 and 8 show the mean income for 1982 graduates in 1983, 1984 and 1985. After three years the Asian graduates are earning rather less, and the Afro-Caribbean graduates slightly more, than the matched samples of white graduates. However, the relative disadvantage of the Asian graduates in terms of income was in fact greater three years after graduation then it was in the first two years.

A slightly different picture emerges out of the data from the 1984 sample. See Figure 9. Three years after graduating the salaries of the 1984 Asian and Caribbean graduates are at opposite ends of the earning continuum. And if we control for the effect of factors such as gender, subject studied and age, we find that the ethnic minority graduates are still earning slightly more than their matched counterparts: Asian graduates £13 124 (compared with £12 203 in the matched sample) and Afro-Caribbean graduates £10 322 (compared with £10 182 in the matched sample).

These positive findings need to be viewed with some caution. The 'London factor' may have inflated the figures for some ethnic groups, and the numbers of people involved are small in some of the groups. Although the evidence on salaries is not clear-cut, it does suggest that difficulties in obtaining jobs and dissatisfaction with these jobs are not necessarily accompanied by an income disadvantage.

There are other more subjective ways of looking at the 'level' of a particular job. We explored these in several ways. Table 21 presents the responses to three questions in the 1984 and 1985 surveys. The first asked: 'Do you consider that your current work is at the moment your most preferred type of occupation?' The Table shows that, with one exception, the ethnic minority samples are less likely to be in their preferred job – the answers reported in the Table are calculated for those graduates working full-time; without this restriction the percentage of the African sample in their preferred job falls to 54.5 per cent (out of 11 cases) while the matched sample rises to 80 per cent (out of ten cases). If the 1984 and 1985 samples are combined, we have 46 per cent of ethnic minority graduates in their preferred job compared with 61 per cent of the matched samples.

The second question asked: 'Do you consider that your current job is a long term career prospect?' Here the contrast is between African and Caribbean graduates, who are much less likely than

Figure 7   Growth in mean income of 1982 Asian graduates

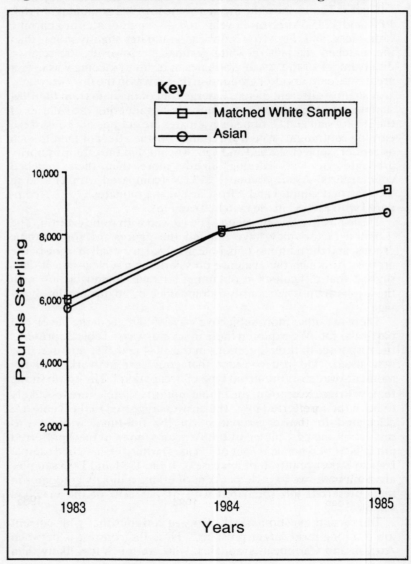

Table 8   Growth in mean income of 1982 Afro Caribbean graduates

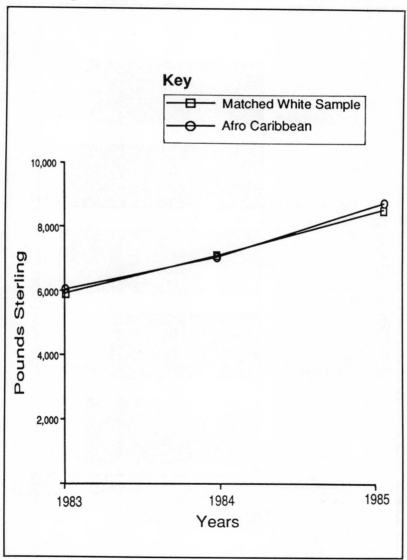

Figure 9   Salaries of the 1984 graduates three years on, by ethnic origin

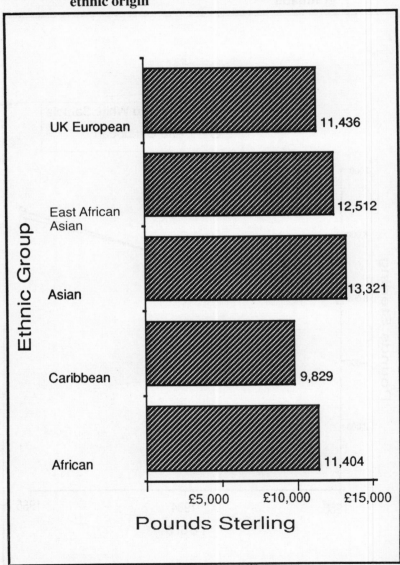

Table 21 **Quality of employment of graduates in full-time work, by ethnic origin (1984 and 1985 samples)**

	Preferred job %	Long term job %	Overqualified for job %	No.
1984 sample				
Asian	46.3	47.5	26.8	40/41
Matched	73.2	47.2	25.0	53/52
Afro-Caribbean	39.1	42.9	45.5	21/22
Matched	58.3	57.1	38.1	21
1985 sample				
Asian	42.1	39.5	38.5	38
Matched	54.8	33.3	40.5	42
East African Asian	53.3	60.0	40.0	15
Matched	78.6	50.0	21.4	14
Caribbean	38.5	15.4	84.6	13
Matched	88.9	55.6	37.5	9
African	80.0	40.0	20.0	5
Matched	77.8	66.7	22.2	9

their matched samples to consider their jobs as long term prospects, and Asian graduates who, compared to their matched group, are slightly more likely to consider them to be long term prospects.

This trend is repeated in the responses to the third question: 'Do you feel that you are overqualified or underqualified for the work that you do?' Caribbean graduates are much more likely to feel overqualified; so too are East African Asians, but the same proportions of other Asians and Africans as their matched samples appear to feel overqualified.

Considering all three questions together one might say that all the ethnic minority groups in these samples have greater difficulty in finding their preferred job and, in the case of Caribbean graduates, the failure to do so seems to result in jobs that do not hold long-term prospects and for which they feel overqualified. In the case of Asian graduates, missing out on the preferred career does not seem to prevent them finding work with long term prospects. They tend not to feel overqualified, and they are more likely to feel that their education is making a considerable difference to the quality of their work.

Table 22 gives the percentages of the graduates in the 1984 sample who felt that the quality of their current work benefited from their undergraduate studies. These are in line with the more general results on the benefits of higher education which we discussed in chapter three. It should be noted here that the graduates were not being asked about the value of their higher education in obtaining employment, but about its contribution to the work they were actually doing. The results need to be interpreted with some care. They reflect the characteristics of current jobs as much as the nature of the higher education experience, and they represent only perceptions. However, they do reinforce the picture of lower career-related benefits perceived by ethnic minorities.

Promotion prospects and career development

The 1985 survey asked the question: 'Have you received any training that is directed towards future promotion and career development rather than towards skills for your existing job?'. Table 23 presents the percentages of those in full-time employment who have received such training. The largest difference is between the Caribbean sample and its matched group; this supports other evidence which suggests that fewer Caribbean graduates are in jobs that have long-term career prospects. However, some caution is

Table 22   Benefits of undergraduate studies to current work (1984 sample)

	Asian %	Matched %	Afro-Caribbean %	Matched %
None/a little	25.9	21.4	30.4	16.7
Fair amount	40.7	37.5	56.5	58.3
Great amount	33.3	41.1	13.0	25.0
	(54)	(56)	(23)	(24)

Note Figures in brackets are numbers.

Table 23   Graduates in full-time employment who received training for future promotion and career development by ethnic origin (1985 sample)

	Received training	
	%	No.
Asian	41	39
Matched	42.9	42
East African Asian	35.7	14
Matched	35.7	14
Caribbean	30.8	13
Matched	66.7	9
African	40.0	5
Matched	33.3	9

required, as both the matched Caribbean and the African group are characterised by a comparatively large proportion who are not in full-time employment and have had a less satisfactory experience in the labour market.

Graduates were asked to rate their promotion prospects on a five point scale from 0 (zero) for very poor to 5 for very good. This scale has been converted to a score out of one hundred in Table 24. It shows that the 1984 sample of ethnic minority graduates considered their chances of being promoted as being somewhat poorer than did their matched counterparts. The 1985 survey shows a more complicated picture. The five (out of 13) African graduates who were working full-time rated their promotion prospects highly. This contrasts with the six Caribbean graduates (out of 13) in full-time employment who rated their employment prospects as being very bad.

The Asian graduates have a slightly higher score, and, although they were less likely to describe their promotion chances as good or very good, they were much less likely than their matched group to describe their chances as very bad. The East African Asians had a lower score for the opposite reason – none described his or her chances as being 'very good' whereas 36 per cent of the matched sample thought they had 'very good' promotion opportunities.

Table 24   Chances of promotion, by ethnic origin (1984 and 1985 samples)

Year of graduation	Ethnic group	Mean score*
1984	Asian	54
	Matched	65
	Afro Caribbean	58
	Matched	62
1985	Asian	51
	Matched	46
	East African Asian	45
	Matched	59
	Caribbean	31
	Matched	72
	African	75
	Matched	53

* Scores are rated on a five point scale from zero for very poor to five for very good.

Overall, the ethnic minority sample had a promotion score of 46 compared to the matched sample's score of 52.

The graduates were asked if they had applied, or been considered, for promotion by their present employers. As Table 25 shows, only 25 per cent of ethnic minority graduates had been considered for promotion compared with 42 per cent of the matched sample. The difference narrows if we consider the percentages of those who have actually been promoted, but a nine per cent promotion gap remains.

Failure to be promoted was an important source of the dissatisfaction expressed by the graduates who were interviewed. Those who were most dissatisfied with their careers were those who had joined companies as graduate recruits with high expectations of promotion and who now felt that they were being overlooked.

Take for instance at work after I had been there six months and my probation had finished. There was a guy, a white guy who

Table 25   Applications for promotion and actual promotions in current employment, by ethnic origin (1985 sample)

	Applied/ Considered for promotion %	Promoted %	No.
Asian	31	23	39
Matched	34	26	50
East African			
Asian	24	24	17
Matched	64	43	14
Caribbean	7	13	15
Matched	39	23	13
African	30	30	10
Matched	56	56	9
All ethnic			
minority	25	22	81
All matched	42	31	86

joined after me, younger than I am, with the same qualifications as me who was appointed to be a supervisor. It's not that I'm not capable of doing the job, I've got the qualifications to prove it etc, yet here I am, just overlooked. . . . Some of my friends think that I am real impatient, but I don't think so. If you have any sort of potential it should be made use of, and it hasn't been made use of in my case. And it has reached a point when I think I can't be bothered. . . . I try not to say it's because I'm black because the first thing that people say is 'Oh she's got a chip on her shoulder', so you can't say that. I would never say it to anyone at work because that's what would happen. [Afro-Caribbean female]

This woman was working for a bank in the City, but similar complaints were made by graduates who had been employed for their technical expertise, but appeared to be excluded from promotion into a more managerial capacity:

69

Everything I've got I have asked for, they have not offered it free to me. When I had the interview with the company they told me within two years at most I would be promoted. Two years went by and nothing happened. The company is split up into groups. I went to see my group manager and he just said to me that he had never said anything to me about promotion within two years, and then he said to me, 'Don't come into my office asking for promotion!'. Then I handed my CV in to the other groups and, because of my experience, another manager offered me a rise in promotion and an increase in salary, subject to the work I'd done after two months of training. Two months later, he tried his best, but the company wouldn't give the promotion. That's when I started looking for other jobs, and then I handed my resignation in. It was then that they decided I was worth giving the money to. [Indian male]

This may be an example of straightforward bad management rather than racial discrimination, though the two are typically found together. What is clear from our interviews is that those ethnic minority graduates who worked for large electronics firms in a technical capacity were extremely disappointed with their career progress to date.

What the interviews revealed was that the graduates' ethnic origin was almost always an issue, even in situations where it did not prejudice the person's chances. In the next example, the graduate had resigned following a dispute with the new head.

In the jobs that I have held I haven't experienced it [discrimination]. When applying for jobs I can't be sure, I sometimes feel that it may be. Obviously, my name. In fact I was extremely fortunate with _____ when I was taken on. I said to the head of marketing, 'tell me frankly, what about my colour, is that part of the consideration . . . I will be meeting customers of yours', and he said, 'well, it would be silly to say that it wasn't a consideration, but I decided that if it was going to put our customers off then we would be better off without them'. Which was extremely reassuring. Unfortunately, he is no longer head of marketing. [East African Asian]

In some situations the interaction between ethnic origin and career can be quite complex. Thus, for a teacher wishing to further the education of his or her ethnic group, this may be a central consideration in making a career choice; and a school without any ethnic minority members of staff may look favourably upon an ethnic minority applicant out of a vague sense that an all white staff is undesirable. However, the organisation of such a school both in its day-to-day activities and in its promotion prospects can repel an otherwise committed teacher.

Because my (PGCE) course had been so challenging in terms of the multicultural aspect, and because I'd done teaching practice in ILEA, I decided that they were the sorts of schools [to work in] *– there were really exciting things going on. I felt I could use my talents best in a multiracial school, particularly working with black children. That is what I wanted to do. I'm not saying I don't want to work with white children, but I think I have far more to offer black children. But the school I went to was not challenging at all. Social studies was seen as a subject for so called 'thick kids'. It was only done at CSE; it was not considered to be a valuable exam subject. I was the only black teacher in the school. There were about five black children. . . . The staff were very old; it was so traditional, so removed from what I'd done on my teaching practice that I realised that after about a term I hated it. I thought at first it was just a case of settling in, but I realised it wasn't going to change. I gave in my notice in May without having another job arranged.* [Afro-Caribbean female]

This graduate found another school, where she was given more responsibility and was in a more supportive atmosphere. However, doubts about her future prospects remained:

[In] *different schools that I've been in, whether on teaching practice or actually teaching, I see black teachers, very good black teachers, on the very junior Scale 1 positions, who have been there quite a long time, and I don't see that I'm going to be particularly any different. So, although I want to make teaching a career, I'm not prepared to stay in an organisation that doesn't value what I'm doing and which doesn't recognise that with promotion . . . When I've been teaching for three or four years I* am *going to expect more, and I don't think that more will be given me.* [Afro-Caribbean female]

The interviews revealed two types of successful career. First, there were those who through professional advancement or self-employment had achieved a level of independence at work which placed them above prejudice: the pharmacist who hoped to run her own shop in the near future seemed to be pleased with her career progress to date; similarly the graduate who, with his parents, ran a sub-post office enjoyed his work and seemed unperturbed by occasional racist insults.

> *Because we get all sorts in* [the post office] *there has to be someone who, in their anger say 'You black this or . . .' but I think that is more heat of the moment than prejudice. I mean, in anger sometimes I'd probably think the same thing. We put it down and laugh about it. The door is always open, if they want to come in it's up to them – money has no colour.* [Asian male]

The second type of successful career was where professional skill and ethnic background were complementary, and the work fitted in with a wider sense of social commitment. The teacher quoted above may be considered to fall within this category. So too would the graduate working in a London borough's Women's Unit:

> *I enjoy my work tremendously. I do a lot of voluntary work in my spare time and I'm able to do that because I'm a resident of the borough. So I go wearing that cap rather than as a council employee. But I find a lot of it links in to the work I'm doing anyway, so it's an added bonus. They may be little factors to some, but they were crucial to me when I was considering working in the borough.* [Asian female, educated in the Caribbean]

The voluntary work – counselling with the Samaritans and on a victim support scheme – also made use of some of the skills acquired in gaining her two degrees in psychology.

Similarly, the graduate working for a housing association enjoyed the work and found her background an advantage:

> *I think it has been* [an advantage], *truthfully. I think when I got this job they were looking for someone from an ethnic minority group because a lot of their tenants are Asian . . . and I speak Gujarati as well and that was certainly a great help.* [Asian female]

Effects of ethnicity on career

Graduates in the 1984 and 1985 samples were asked which factors helped or hindered them in finding a suitable job. Table 26 shows the replies of four groups of graduates in the 1984 sample. The replies by ethnic minority graduates and their UK European equivalents were remarkably similar, except that both Afro-Caribbean and Asian graduates were far more likely to see their ethnic origin as hindering them in their search for employment. In addition Asian graduates were more likely than their matched counterparts to say that their pre-college education and previous experience had not helped them to find suitable employment.

For the 1985 sample, previous experience and ethnic origin continued to be important. In addition a small, but consistent, 14 per cent of Asian graduates thought that family responsibilities had been a hindrance in their career. See Table 27.

These are graduates' perceptions and it is possible that they are mistaken; racial discrimination or 'lack of experience' may be explanations given to explain labour market difficulties the causes of which lie elsewhere. Thus graduates may say lack of experience has hindered them when in fact it is racial discrimination – or vice versa. However, a more interesting question is raised if both are assumed to be true; namely, why do ethnic minority graduates appear to have less beneficial previous experience?

Pharmacy

In our previous report for the CRE, the relatively large numbers of Asian graduates in pharmacy enabled us to pay particular attention to the experiences of this group of graduates. We have been able to repeat the exercise using the 1984 sample.

Twenty-four graduates with CNAA degrees in pharmacy described their ethnic origins as Asian or Afro-Asian. We examined their experiences in the labour market compared with UK Europeans who had undertaken the same course.

It was originally intended to compare the experiences of these 24 graduates with those of all UK European pharmacy graduates. This approach, however, was rejected, because the gender composition of the two groups was very different: 58.9 per cent of UK European but only 16.7 per cent of Asian pharmacists were women. This is

Table 26   Factors determining success in the labour market, by ethnic origin (1984 sample)

	Afro-Caribbean			Matched			Asian			Matched		
	Help %	Neutral %	Hinder %	Help %	Neutral %	Hinder %	Help %	Neutral %	Hinder %	Help %	Neutral %	Hinder %
Degree subject	58.3	29.2	12.5	50.0	37.5	12.5	80.0	15.6	4.4	89.8	37.5	2.0
Degree class	33.3	41.7	25.0	25.0	62.5	12.5	32.6	54.3	13.0	26.5	62.5	8.2
College attended	8.3	87.5	4.2	4.2	95.8	—	4.5	81.8	13.6	14.3	95.8	8.2
Pre-college education	20.0	68.0	12.0	20.8	70.8	8.3	13.6	75.0	11.4	26.5	70.8	8.2
Previous experience	56.0	28.0	16.0	62.5	29.2	8.3	27.3	54.5	18.2	40.8	29.2	4.1
Gender	8.7	78.3	13.0	8.7	87.0	4.3	—	93.2	6.8	12.5	87.0	—
Ethnicity	8.7	39.1	52.2	4.3	95.7	—	—	68.9	31.1	6.3	95.7	—
Family responsibility	4.2	95.8	—	4.2	95.8	—	4.4	82.2	13.3	4.1	93.9	2.0

Table 27 Effects of previous experience and ethnic origin on career (1985 sample)

	Asian %	Matched %	East African Asian %	Matched %	Caribbean %	Matched %	African %	Matched %
Previous experience								
Helped	26.5	34.0	31.3	77.8	55.6	70.6	45.5	62.5
Neutral	44.9	41.5	37.5	16.7	11.1	23.5	36.4	25.0
Hindered	28.6	24.5	31.3	5.6	33.3	5.9	18.2	12.5
	(49)	(53)	(16)	(18)	(18)	(17)	(11)	(8)
Ethnic origin								
Helped	4.2	5.7	4.2	5.7	31.6	5.9	—	—
Neutral	66.7	94.3	62.5	88.2	31.6	94.1	81.8	100.0
Hindered	29.2	—	31.3	5.9	36.8	—	18.2	—
	(48)	(53)	(16)	(17)	(19)	(17)	(11)	(7)

Note Figures in brackets are numbers.

important because the careers of men and women tend to be very different from one another. Research (Chapman 1988) suggests that women tend to earn less and obtain employment in lower status jobs than men, and failure to correct for this imbalance could, therefore, have led to biased conclusions. Hence, it was decided to compare the experiences of Asian graduates with their matched counterparts only.

Table 28 shows the employment status of the two groups of pharmacists in April 1985, 1986 and 1987. (The Table was adjusted to exclude those not seeking work.) It can be seen that almost all the Asian graduates and their matched counterparts were in employment at these three dates. Two Asian graduates were, however, in full-time education in April 1986 and April 1987. The main difference between the two groups lies in the proportions who were self-employed. Asian pharmacy graduates were far more likely to be self-employed three years after graduation than their UK European equivalents, even though they had started out working for someone else in the year after graduation.

Looking at the various indicators of job quality, we find that only 50.0 per cent of *all* Asian pharmacy graduates (including the self-employed), but 82.6 per cent of their matched equivalents were in their preferred occupations. Asian graduates who were not self-employed tended to work for smaller firms than their matched counterparts, and thus 45.5 per cent of Asians (11) but only 19 per cent of their matched counterparts (21) were employed by firms

Table 28   Employment status of Asian pharmacy graduates (1984 sample)

	April 1985		April 1986		April 1987	
	Asian %	Matched %	Asian %	Matched %	Asian %	Matched %
Employed	100.0	95.8	69.6	100.0	36.4	87.5
Self-employed	—	—	17.4	—	54.5	12.5
Full-time study	—	4.2	8.4	—	9.1	—
Unemployed	—	—	4.3	—	—	—
	(23)	(24)	(23)	(24)	(22)	(24)

Note Figures in brackets are numbers.

76

with fewer than 20 employees. Asian pharmacy graduates who were employees rated their promotion prospects as being far worse than did their UK European equivalents: the mean scores on a scale from 0 (very poor) to 100 (very good) were 53.3 and 69.0 respectively.

Although these data can be taken as evidence that Asian pharmacy graduates are employed in lower-status occupations than their matched counterparts, these findings are not supported by other evidence. No major differences existed in the proportions needing a degree for entry into their occupations, and Asians were marginally less likely to feel overqualified. Moreover, among the 13 Asians and 16 UK Europeans who answered the question, Asians (mean income £16 923) were actually earning £2775 a year more than UK Europeans (mean income £14 148).

Conclusions

The fortunes of the Asian pharmacy graduates represent something of a special case, but one which does illustrate some of the contradictory features of graduate employment for ethnic minorities. There is not a problem of long-term unemployment, and in terms of salary, ethnic minority graduates appear in most cases to be doing at least as well as their white counterparts. On the other hand, it is quite clear that ethnic minority graduates encounter special difficulties in obtaining jobs and are generally less satisfied with the jobs they eventually obtain. They are less likely to be considered for promotion and less likely to receive training specially geared towards promotion. And they *feel* that race is a factor that works against them at all stages of the job-finding process.

What do ethnic minority graduates do about this? We have seen how they are likely to invest in additional education through postgraduate study; this is in keeping with the comments made in several interviews about the importance that graduates believed *should* be attached to educational qualifications by employers. Unfortunately the graduate labour market in Britain does not operate in this way. In most employment areas recruiters appear to be looking for sets of personal attributes and skills which are difficult to operationalise and difficult to counter. Thus, the graduate recruitment process remains shrouded in some mystery. The graduate is never quite sure what he or she has to do in order to be successful; nor does the graduate know what she or he has done wrong when rejected. In such circumstances, and in particular when the labour market is generally difficult, graduates are more likely to perceive discrimination and employers can more easily profess their innocence.

Ethnic minorities appear to have a greater faith in the power of qualifications than the facts of the labour market would justify. But when that faith is undermined, as in many of the interviews it appeared to have been, what can graduates do? The pharmacists again provide the clue to a practical answer: they can become self-employed, and, in the case of the pharmacists, successfully so. Undoubtedly, cultural factors combine with labour market difficulties in increasing the attractiveness of self-employment. It is not an option so readily available to graduates from all subject areas. Nor can it really be considered a desirable option if it is a response to discrimination and unfairness by employers of graduates.

Ethnic minorities, along with some other groups, appear to be on the margins of the graduate labour market. When the labour market opportunities are few, it is the ethnic minorities, mature graduates, women graduates, and non-university graduates who appear to suffer most. The fact that the next few years are likely to bring an overall shortage of graduates may reduce the likelihood of actual hardship, but it will not remove the inequalities of opportunity for well-qualified graduates from the 'wrong' social or ethnic backgrounds.

Chapter 5

Institutional Perspectives

Attempting to gain a complete and accurate view of how ethnic background interacts with education to produce distinct patterns of career progress involves piecing together different kinds of evidence. This has so far consisted of descriptions by graduates of their own experiences in education and in finding and doing a job. However, interviews were also carried out with other participants in, and observers of, these educational and labour market processes. Careers advisors were well placed to give an assessment, albeit one influenced by a distinctive professional world view. Useful accounts were also gained from other academic and administrative staff in the higher education institutions we visited.

Finding employment

The interviewees' responses generally supported the survey findings by suggesting that ethnic minority graduates experienced more difficulties in finding employment than white graduates from the same courses. The following were the principal and clearest examples offered:

1. One careers advisor noted problems for ethnic minority graduates from computer sciences. When graduates from one particular year of this course were surveyed, over half of the 14 unemployed students were ethnic minority, even though ethnic minority students were a minority of the graduates as a whole.
2. Ethnic minority graduates in business studies obtained jobs fairly easily, but these tended to be less well-paid and in different sectors than the jobs of white graduates. Interviewees from the London institutions also commented on the fact that the prospects of ethnic minority graduates in these subjects for employment in the City itself were noticeably less good than those for white graduates.
3. Asian engineering graduates experienced more difficulties in obtaining employment than their white counterparts.

4. A phrase used by one of the careers advisors was typical of the responses made by the others in describing the employment prospects of the ethnic minority graduates:

   They have to cast their nets wider, make more applications, and take longer to find employment than the white graduates.

There was one marked *inversion* of these typical patterns in the case of a college training primary teachers. The subsequent employment of all their ethnic minority students was closely monitored by the course director and the head of department, both of whom felt they could claim with some confidence that, if anything, the employment prospects of their ethnic minority graduates were better than those of their white students. Both of these respondents attributed this to a considerable demand for ethnic minority teachers coupled with a relatively short supply, and suggested that this particular course provided a significant proportion of the total number of ethnic minority graduates entering primary education each year.

Subject differences

As a general determinant of employment expectations the influence of the course taken would appear to be paramount. Careers and academic staff agreed in seeing this as the major determinant of the employment expectations of their ethnic minority students. Thus, as with actual employment outcomes, the employment expectations of ethnic minority students more closely resemble those of white students on the same course than members of the same ethnic minority group on different courses. This also suggests that students' and staff's knowledge and impressions of the employment outcomes of graduates from specific courses are major determinants of employment expectations. Ethnic minority graduates from business studies or engineering, for example, were perceived as having higher expectations of finding suitable employment more quickly than ethnic minority graduates in the social sciences, arts and humanities.

In looking for explanations of the employment difficulties faced by ethnic minority graduates it is appropriate to consider again the perceived subject distribution of ethnic minority students in higher education institutions. Perceived is the operative word, as only one of the institutions visited practised systematic ethnic monitoring based on admission data and annual registration forms. Thus the observations were based on impressionistic or incomplete data.

In engineering and science ethnic minority students were thought to be concentrated more in computer science and chemistry than in the other sciences. The large majority were Asian, and in engineering almost all the Asian students were male. This reflects the gender balance for these courses as a whole, but the Asian males in engineering are often a few years older than their white counterparts. In the other sciences, compared with engineering, the proportions of women appeared to be higher, and the proportions of mature students lower, among the Asians.

Like their white counterparts, almost all the Asian students in engineering and science appeared to be conventionally qualified in terms of 'A' level or equivalent qualifications.

Engineering and science students were contrasted with social science students. Ethnic minority students in the social sciences were perceived as more likely to be Afro-Caribbean, female, older, non-conventionally qualified and working class. However, there was also course-related variation within the social sciences. Sociology, social studies and social work all seemed to recruit substantial proportions of ethnic minorities in general, and the 'typical' older, female, Afro-Caribbean student in particular. In economics, geography and town planning, the students tended to be predominantly white, middle class, and conventionally aged and qualified.

In business studies, arts and humanities there were only small proportions of ethnic minority students on degree courses, and intra ethnic variations were unclear. However, the ethnic minority students in arts and humanities were perceived as being Afro-Caribbean rather than Asian, and predominantly female. Interviewees perceived the overwhelming majority of students on these courses as white, middle-class, rather 'home counties', conventionally aged and conventionally qualified, albeit without high enough 'A' level grades for the university places that were undoubtedly their first choice. This was felt to be particularly true for the female students. In general, there seemed to be a suggestion that the student composition of the business studies and arts courses consisted predominantly of white, middle-class school-leavers who had missed out on university, with the males opting more for business studies and the females more for arts and humanities.

Explanations of these variations focused on locality and admission procedure in addition to student preference. Polytechnics whose locality included areas with high proportions of ethnic minority people attracted students from these areas, and indeed ethnic minority students from other areas may have been attracted by the distinctive cosmopolitan culture of such institutions. One of the colleges studied was based on two sites: a city centre campus, which attracted a high proportion of ethnic minority students, and a rural campus 15 miles away, which attracted very few. However, the different proportions of ethnic minority students taking these courses seemed to be associated with consistent differences in admissions policies. The rurally located courses attached greater importance to 'A' level scores as a criterion for admission, and generally admitted a smaller proportion of entrants with non-standard qualifications.

Overall, respondents felt that these variations were closely related to the more flexible admissions policies operated in the social sciences and the more rapid development of access courses for non-standard entrants in these areas.

The explanations of careers advisors

Ethnic minority graduates were considered to face particular difficulties in the labour market. Explanations offered as to why this was so were not intended to deny that some graduates would encounter racism in their search for work. They were complementary explanations rather than alternatives, drawing attention to processes that compound the existence of direct prejudice. In presenting these explanations careers advisors expressed what are perhaps the two central features of their professional outlook. First, that discrimination was not in anybody's interest, as it restricted the pool of highly skilled personnel available to employers; and second, that their orientation was one of counselling individuals, each of whom has a distinct set of characteristics, abilities and expectations. Thus they tended to focus on the graduate's self-presentation and confidence-building rather than on external factors.

However, there was an awareness of such factors. Thus, interviewees at all the institutions felt that whatever the problems encountered by ethnic minority graduates in entering labour markets, these were compounded if these graduates were female, and if they were older than the conventional graduates. (One of the graduates we interviewed referred to the additional problems of being a mature student.) Several respondents at the London polytechnics suggested that Asian females, for example, experienced more difficulties in finding employment than Asian males, and that the employment prospects of Afro-Caribbean graduates in the social sciences were reduced further by the fact that they were typically older, with non-standard qualifications, often from working-class backgrounds and sometimes with domestic responsibilities.

Careers advisors identified several other factors that differentiated between ethnic minority and white students on the same courses, and these perceptions tended to be shared by academic staff. In general, ethnic minority students were seen to have lower expectations and higher anxiety about their employment prospects than white students on the same courses. Interviewees suggested that ethnic minority students, and especially ethnic minority female students, may be prepared in advance to set their employment aspirations lower than their white counterparts and to accept more readily a job which they would not necessarily see as the one they would most prefer. However, the ambitions of ethnic minority and white students on the same course may not initially be different from each other but may become more different during the actual experience of applying for jobs.

All the careers advisors felt that ethnic minority students were more anxious about their employment prospects, and anticipated more difficulties in finding suitable employment than white students on the same courses. All the careers officers, apart from the one at the college, felt that they saw a higher proportion of ethnic minority than white students from each course and explained this largely in terms of the former's higher anxiety and lower self-confidence about obtaining employment. Even the college careers officer felt that ethnic minority students displayed these traits, even if they were not clearly reflected in a higher proportion of ethnic minority undergraduates making use of the careers service. One of the careers advisors at a London polytechnic went so far as to suggest that the higher anxiety and lower self-confidence of ethnic minority students were an expression of their more vocational orientation to higher education in general and were causes of their underrepresentation on the less vocational courses in the social sciences, arts and humanities.

All of the careers advisors tended to suggest that ethnic minority students in general experienced more difficulties in self-presentation and self-projection than white students, and that this was related to problems of self-expression, both oral and written, and to general problems of language and communication. Several of the interviewees attempted to support this impression by suggesting that Asian students experienced particular difficulties in this area, and that Asian students raised and educated in Britain experienced significantly fewer problems than Asian students who had received the bulk of their pre-college education overseas. Again the careers advisors tended to suggest that ethnic minority students' perceptions of their own problems in these areas, and their anticipation of related problems in job applications and interviews, were a significant factor in bringing them to seek advice and assistance from careers services.

These factors of lower employment expectations, higher anxiety and problems with communication, self-expression and self-projection were seen by careers advisors as contributing to a lower self esteem among ethnic minority students. This general notion of lower self-esteem and lack of self-confidence seemed for careers advisors to crystallise the situation of ethnic minority students as a 'problem' to which the careers professionals could address themselves particularly.

These comments, observations and perceptions of careers officers, generally supported by those of academic staff, suggest that it is not just the 'objective' ethnic and demographic characteristics and educational qualifications of ethnic minority students which can disadvantage their search for employment, but also 'subjective orientations' which might be perceived by themselves and others as 'personality traits'. However, it must be emphasised that these traits, just as much as their demographic characteristics and educational qualifications, are socially constructed products of the social experience, especially the pre-college experience, of ethnic minority students. Moreover, such traits as lower expectations, higher anxiety, and lack of self-confidence would be quite 'rational' responses to their experiences of job-seeking as students and as graduates. Different, more favourable experiences would lead to correspondingly different traits.

At the same time, these observations allow a clearer appreciation of how some of the difficulties facing ethnic minority students in their search for employment might be alleviated within higher education. In particular, they provide a clearer appreciation of the context within which these difficulties may be addressed through careers advice and guidance.

As well as the general assumptions made by careers staff about ethnic minority students in general, their professional predisposition to consider the individual characteristics and needs of each student led them to emphasise that the age and sex of each student, their particular course and qualifications, and their personal orientations and circumstances were at least as important as their ethnic origin. At the same time, however, their comments revealed course-specific clusters of characteristics which influenced the employment prospects and expectations of ethnic minority students, and the sorts of advice and guidance which could be offered to them.

Thus, the careers advisors tended to suggest that:

1. Female Asian students may well have lower employment expectations and be less 'assertive' and persistent in their search for employment than Asian males from the same courses.

2. Afro-Caribbean students quite often tended to be older than both Asian and white students. This presented them with particular difficulties in seeking employment, and was also indicative of the fact that a significant proportion of Afro-Caribbean students had entered higher education as non-standard entrants from working-class backgrounds and from previous working-class employment. For the careers advisors this meant that Afro-Caribbean students were particularly likely to need advice on a general reorientation towards the world of middle-class employment, for example in making job applications and managing job interviews.

3. Afro-Caribbean students in the social sciences were particularly likely to display these characteristics and to experience these difficulties. Moreover, these difficulties were likely to be compounded further by the fact that a high proportion of them were female, many with domestic responsibilities circumscribing the range of jobs for which they could apply.

The practice of careers staff appeared to reflect their general assumptions about ethnic minority students and their awareness of intra ethnic variations. Thus, the work of the careers staff appeared to display the following characteristics:

1. The careers officers displayed a marked orientation towards counselling students rather than finding them particular jobs in the way associated with job centres or employment agencies. They saw their own roles as encouraging their 'clients' to raise their employment expectations, self-esteem and self-confidence, and to value their previous work experience, waged or unwaged, in their job applications and interviews. They felt that this general orientation toward their work with students was particularly important with ethnic minority students, and with female ethnic minority students in particular. This approach was felt to be even more important for female Afro-Caribbean students in social science, many of whom had previously worked at non-graduate levels in the health and social services, or had other previous experience which was likely to be valued by prospective employers more highly than they realised.

2. While there was some indication that careers advisors were running workshops in these areas for students as a whole, or for students from particular courses, there seemed to be no such workshop sessions for ethnic minorities in particular. Help and guidance which was felt particularly useful for ethnic minority students seemed to come primarily in the work done by careers advisors with individual students who came to see them. The careers staff (all of them white) in general seemed reluctant to 'single out' ethnic minority students for special treatment. In this respect, and in many others, all would have welcomed the advice of specialist careers officers for ethnic minority students. Only one institution, one of the London polytechnics, received support from a part-time specialist careers advisor. In general, the careers officers reported that although they had requested more help in this area, institutional resources had not been forthcoming. They were likely to rely for help and guidance upon specialised units established to deal with equal opportunities and ethnic minority issues more generally.

3. All the careers advisors felt that the sorts of advice and guidance appropriate to ethnic minority students could be handled particularly effectively through incorporation into the 'mainstream' teaching process of each particular course. However, while they saw increasing tendencies in this direction, with closer cooperation between careers staff and

academic teaching staff, it was felt that initiatives in this potentially very helpful area were proceeding much too slowly.

Work experience in higher education

One final topic covered both by the interviews with staff and with graduates and by the questionnaire surveys was the experience of ethnic minority graduates on courses with sandwich or work experience components.

Work experience is an essential feature of many polytechnic courses, providing a source of contacts, practical experience and general education. At its best it can be a valuable asset to a graduate seeking employment; at the very least it gives the graduate something tangible to talk about in an interview. Work placement experience in a prestigious company is likely to be of considerable benefit. Thus one graduate said:

The time at ICI was very good, in the lab and socially as well. It was the first time I was on a salary. Again you are put into another community. It's not academic altogether, not everyone you are working with is qualified. You are living with someone totally new – you are sharing with them. [East African male]

Evidence from a variety of studies (such as CNAA, 1984) suggests that sandwich placements generally improve students' employment prospects. This would confirm the observations of the careers officers noted above to the effect that employment prospects are better for ethnic minority students on sandwich degrees, and that they are less likely to see ethnic minority students from such courses than their peers on non-sandwich courses. However, the evidence suggests two principal ways in which the actual placement experience of ethnic minority students may *not* enhance employment prospects to the same extent as it does for white students on the same degrees. First, it may be more difficult for ethnic minority students to obtain satisfactory placements. Second, experience of racial discrimination during placement could shake the confidence of ethnic minority students and produce a lowering of career ambitions.

With such issues in mind, interviews were conducted at one college with tutors responsible for finding and supervising sandwich placements for trainee teachers and other students. Particular attention was paid to the question of whether racial prejudice had affected the finding of suitable placements or the students' placement experiences.

The responses of the tutors indicated that there was no more difficulty in finding suitable placements for ethnic minority than for white students. However, the interviewees felt that the generally favourable situation for finding student placements could be related to the sorts of employers approached by the college. The placement tutors and their students were looking almost exclusively for placements in the public and voluntary sectors within the local conurbation. In this area, the local authorities had clearly articulated and pursued equal opportunity policies, and this had affected their own receptiveness toward ethnic minority students on placement.

However, the interviewees suggested that the relative ease in finding placements did not guarantee the absence of racism during placement periods. Student teachers certainly appeared to experience it from parents and children, and occasionally complained about racial harassment from colleagues. The non-school placement tutors felt that this sort of harassment, quite frequently from clients or customers, and less frequently from colleagues, was also experienced by their students, though to a less publicised degree. In these non-school areas racial harassment was assumed to be more diffuse and less commented upon by the students. In the last three years there had been only one case which raised sufficient attention, after the student's complaint, for the student to be withdrawn from the placement. This was a case of a student based in a youth assessment centre who experienced severe racial abuse from the centre's 'clients'. Again, this was seen as a fairly typical experience in which racial abuse and harassment was not so much likely to come from the students' colleagues as from members of the public, clients or customers over whom the placement organisation frequently had little direct control.

One further feature noted by the non-school placement tutors was the tendency for ethnic minority students to seek out areas which they perceived as relatively safe or welcoming and which might simultaneously enhance their prospects of future employment. Thus, ethnic minority students were likely to seek placements in organisations and community agencies dealing specifically with ethnic issues and ethnic minority communities or catering for and already staffed by members of ethnic minorities. The one student (young Asian female) currently placed in a bank, and therefore, atypically, in a private sector commercial organisation, was in a local Asian bank.

Our interviews with ethnic minority graduates and our survey data indicate some of the problems faced in obtaining suitable work experience placements. One of the ethnic minority graduates we interviewed reported how his first year's 'industrial experience' was in a technical college where the students who did not actually get any training in industry were given an electronics and manufacturing course instead. The student claimed that most of the students so placed were from ethnic minorities or from overseas.

This graduate played an active role in finding his second placement. However, not all graduates had the experience and contacts to do so and were thus heavily dependent on their polytechnic to find suitable placements.

It was supposed to be a sandwich course . . . I put in to do work within management training in a large department store but the choices I got – it wasn't available. They were asking me for contacts. I didn't have any contacts. In the end I went and worked for a health authority getting training from the admin based training . . . salaries and wages and that sort of thing. That wasn't really what I put in for. It was a matter of this or nothing. Really you had to find something for yourself, and I wasn't really in a position. I didn't have any contacts really. If you had contacts, provided the college thought it was based loosely on the course you were doing, the college were prepared to let you do it. It got to that kind of stage. This was in 1980–81. [Afro-Caribbean male]

The other problem faced by students in finding a sandwich placement was distance from home. This could be a particular problem for ethnic minorities, who, in addition to being away from their families, could face hostility and racism in an unknown town. One graduate we interviewed had to take the first job offered after finishing his course in order to gain the work experience necessary to graduate – experience that should have been achieved through placements during the course.

Most of the industrial training was very far away from home. I didn't want to leave home for all that time. We were supposed to do three in our four years. I think it was 52 weeks altogether. I did the first part. I didn't do the second and the third. . . . In the second period I was offered training in Harwich. That, I thought, was no way on – it was over two hours drive or by train. I said to

89

my tutor 'look it's too far away', and the reply I got was that it was difficult enough getting somewhere never mind being fussy over it as well. That's what happened in the third sandwich as well. The third one was in Manchester, a company that makes electrical modules. That I refused because I just could not get accommodation. I stayed a couple of days at the YMCA. . . . I was not familiar with the area. Nobody knew me up there. . . . I was unemployed (when should have been doing sandwich) and that was why I had to finish my training up here. That was the main reason that I took the first job that I was offered. [Indian male]

The sample of 1985 graduates were asked how satisfied they were with the work and training given on their work experience placement. See Table 29, which shows that ethnic minority graduates were less likely to be satisfied (78% compared to 85%). In particular, nine per cent were *very* dissatisfied with the training they were given.

Conclusions

The problems encountered by ethnic minorities on work placements to some extent foreshadowed the kinds of problems they would encounter when seeking full-time employment. They obtained placements – as they would eventually obtain jobs – but sometimes with difficulty, and they were quite likely to encounter racism, often quite outside of the control of the employer.

In looking at ethnic minority employment from the point of view of higher education institutions, we can see something of the

Table 29 Satisfaction with work experience placements (1985 sample)

	Ethnic minorities %	Matched %
Very dissatisfied	9	0
Dissatisfied	13	15
Satisfied	50	58
Very satisfied	28	29

constraints under which these institutions try to tackle the problem. Faced with a perception of what employers are looking for, careers advisors must either try to convert students into the 'desired product', or seek to match students with 'appropriate' employment settings. The latter runs the risk of depressing aspirations while the former runs the risk of 'blaming the victim'. Therefore, it becomes important for careers advisors, individually and collectively through bodies such as the Association of Graduate Careers Advisory Services (AGCAS), to challenge the way in which the labour market works and to work with employers of graduates to remove the prejudices and stereotypes that disfavour the ethnic minority graduate.

Chapter 6

Conclusions and Recommendations

Ethnic minority groups are unevenly represented in British higher education. Participation among Asian groups is comparable to that of UK Europeans, but it is low among Caribbeans. Our survey data suggest that ethnic minorities are unevenly spread within higher education as well. They appear to be heavily concentrated in a limited number of types of courses, mainly in the polytechnics and colleges. Course of study is a crucial determinant of future employment. Thus, employment concentrations tend to follow on from educational concentrations.

There are features of the employment profiles of ethnic minority graduates which cannot be explained in terms of the type of course or institution. These have less to do with the type of work than with the type of employer. Thus, graduates from the Afro-Caribbean community are more likely to find employment in the public sector, and Asian graduates are more likely to be self-employed.

All ethnic minority graduates face a greater likelihood of being unemployed after graduation, and they report more difficulty in finding suitable employment. However, as with all graduates, they are very unlikely to be unemployed in the long term. But although they are ultimately successful in getting a job, they are less likely than white graduates to be satisfied with it, and, although the evidence is not all one way, the quality of job obtained is likely to be inferior to that obtained by a similarly qualified white graduate. In describing the difficulties they encountered in finding suitable employment, the ethnic minority graduates mentioned ethnic origin as the factor which most hindered their search for a job. They felt that it often influenced the conduct and outcome of job interviews. This was supported by the survey evidence, which indicated that the ethnic minorities needed more interviews than white graduates in order to obtain an offer of a job.

Our research has provided strong indication of the success of access policies in institutions of higher education in the polytechnics and colleges sector in extending educational opportunities to minority groups.

Pre-entry access courses, sensitive admissions procedures and a multicultural approach to curriculum planning all contribute to making higher education possible and desirable to ethnic minorities. What is lacking is the consistent implementation of policies of this sort, between sectors of higher education and within higher education institutions. In relation to the latter, it was noteworthy that, even in those institutions with strong and highly visible policies on equal opportunities, only two or three subject departments appeared to be seriously implementing them. This has the effect of channelling students from ethnic minorities into only a limited range of educational opportunities. Employment opportunities are restricted as a consequence.

As we have already emphasised, irrespective of their choice of course, graduates from ethnic minorities face particular difficulties in the labour market. The perception and anticipation of difficulties by the students themselves can lead to a further channelling of job applications towards employers thought to be sympathetic, even if this entails a lowering of aspirations as a consequence. It is not a pleasant experience being rejected for a job, particularly after (sometimes multiple) interviews. And it is an experience that ethnic minority graduates go through more often than their white peers. Hardly surprising then if disillusion is the result.

Members of ethnic minorities tend to place considerable value on education. The ethnic minority graduates in our surveys and interviews expressed considerable satisfaction with their experiences of higher education. Where there was dissatisfaction it was with the rewards provided by the labour market for educational qualifications. For many of the graduates, educational opportunity had proved not to be the avenue towards employment opportunity that they had expected.

To summarise, ethnic minority graduates face greater difficulties in obtaining jobs than other graduates. They obtain less satisfying jobs and find promotion more difficult to obtain. At the individual level, they are not quite sure why this is so. Many suspect discrimination by employers on the basis of ethnic origin, but few can give any direct evidence of discrimination because the whole recruitment process is too often shrouded in secrecy and mystique. Graduates are not sure what criteria are being used, nor how they measure up to them. Educational qualifications and the necessary skills to do the job appear not to be enough. What then is lacking?

Unlike the individual ethnic minority graduate, we have been able to look at the experiences of several hundred graduates. From

93

these it is very difficult to conclude anything but that there is some racial discrimination in the graduate labour market. We have no direct evidence that it is conscious or intentional, but it is difficult to explain in any other way the problems indicated by the surveys and the interviews. We have discussed in this report the role which educational qualifications play in the labour market and the extent to which they need to be coupled with other, perhaps more nebulous, qualities in order to impress the prospective employer. In part, it is an example of the British 'generalist' tradition with its emphasis on the personal and social characteristics of an individual rather than specialist knowledge and certificates. But there are real dangers that this tradition serves to perpetuate existing social hierarchies and is a screen by which socially dominant groups reproduce themselves. Ethnic minority graduates find themselves in a competition for jobs without being told the rules.

Our various pieces of research have perhaps indicated two main things, one positive and one negative. The positive aspect is that members of ethnic minorities appear to benefit enormously from higher education, in personal, educational and employment terms. The negative aspect is that the employment benefits are not as great as they should be; the possession of educational qualifications does not of itself ensure equality of opportunity in the labour market.

We believe that there are a number of things that can and should be done to help improve the employment opportunities of graduates from ethnic minorities. Five of these recommendations are directed towards institutions of higher education, and eight towards employers of graduates.

Recommendations to institutions of higher education

1. Institutions should set out written statements of policy on equal opportunities. Such policies should cover admissions (including appropriate pre-entry access), the educational experiences available to students, and the outcomes of those experiences (including employment outcomes).

2. The policies should be thoroughly implemented in *all* departments and should be monitored by the institution through the collection and analysis of ethnic origin records. The differential

take-up by ethnic minority students of places between various courses does not obviate the need for all course teams to ensure that opportunities are available and publicised to ethnic communities.

3. Institutions should, in their dealings with employers, seek to promote the adoption of good equal opportunity practices, and, in particular, should press employers to be more specific about what they require of prospective employees, to set out clearly the criteria by which applicants will be judged and the methods used to assess applicants against those criteria. This will not only give a greater sense of fairness but will enable students to prepare more effectively for entry into the labour market.

4. Institutions should establish a clear policy regarding employers who give instructions to careers services or agents to discriminate on racial grounds, or put pressure on them to discriminate on racial grounds over placements or permanent employment, including referral of appropriate cases to the CRE. They should actively oppose discriminatory treatment of students on placement and challenge employers who appear to reject students on racial grounds.

5. Institutions should ensure that ethnic minority students are aware of the importance attached by employers to communication and presentational skills, and should provide suitable opportunities for them to acquire these skills. Where appropriate, they should consider the scope for meeting this need sensitively within their overall arrangements for careers counselling and preparation.

6. Institutions should arrange for staff, both specialist careers advisors and others, to receive training in the requirements of a multiracial and multicultural society.

Recommendations to employers

1. In accordance with the *Code of Practice* in employment issued by the CRE, employers should adopt and implement a policy on equality of opportunity and ensure that applicants and others, including higher education institutions, are aware of the

policy. They should monitor the policy by collecting and analysing records on the ethnic origins of applicants and appointees.

2. Employers should bring vacancies to the attention of the widest possible field, where appropriate by widening the range of institutions visited for recruitment purposes to include those with larger numbers of ethnic minority graduates.

3. Employers should set out clearly for the benefit of applicants the criteria against which they will be judged and the methods used for assessing applicants against those criteria; they should ensure that recruitment personnel apply the criteria and methods consistently and fairly.

4. In estimating an individual's potential, employers should consider relative educational achievement. Non-traditional graduates have probably shown greater commitment, self-discipline and endeavour. They may have achieved more in terms of distance travelled than a graduate with the same final qualification but with a more favoured background.

5. Employers should question the use of 'A' and 'O' levels to distinguish between suitable graduates, because it effectively excludes all non-traditional graduates.

6. Employers should not discriminate on grounds of age. Unless they expect employees to remain for 40 years, it usually makes little sense and it disproportionately excludes ethnic minority applicants.

7. Employers should question the use of social activities as an indicator of suitability. They should remember that students from disadvantaged backgrounds (who have probably had to show greater persistance and tenacity in gaining entry to higher education) may consider their education the most pressing activity as an undergraduate.

8. If social activities are considered to be important indicators of suitability, then employers should assess these activities fairly – the secretary of the Islamic society is likely to have shown an equal amount of organisational and social skill as the captain of the rugby team.

Bibliography

Allen, S, Bentley, S and Bornat, J. 1977. *Work, Race and Immigration*. University of Bradford.

Ballard, R and Holden, R. 1975. The employment of coloured graduates in Britain. *New Community*, vol 4, no. 3.

Ballard, R and Vellins, S. 1985. South Asian entrants to British universities: a comparative note. *New Community*, vol 12, no. 2.

Barber, A. 1985. Ethnic origins and economic status. *Employment Gazette*, December 1985.

Blakeney, R and McNaughton, J. 1971. Effects of temporal placement of unfavourable information on decision-making during the selection interview. *Journal of Applied Psychology*, vol 55.

Boys, C and Kirkland, J. 1988. *Degrees of Success: Career aspirations and destinations of a cohort of college, university and polytechnic graduates*. Jessica Kingsley Publishers.

Brennan, J and McGeevor, P. 1987. *Employment of Graduates from Ethnic Minorities*. London: Commission for Racial Equality.

Brennan, J and McGeevor, P. 1988. *Graduates at Work: Degree courses and the labour market*. Jessica Kingsley Publishers.

Brooks, D and Singh, D. 1975. *Aspirations Versus Opportunity: Asian and white school leavers in the Midlands*. The Walsall and Leicester Community Relations Councils.

Brown, C. 1984. *Black and White Britain: The third PSI survey*. London: Heinemann Educational Books.

Chapman, A. 1988. *Just the Ticket? Graduate men and women in the labour market three years after college*. HELM Working Paper 5. Staffordshire Polytechnic.

Collier, J and Burke, A. 1986. Racial and sexual discrimination in the selection of students for London medical schools. *Medical Education*, vol 20.

Commission for Racial Equality. 1987. *Chartered Accountancy Training Contracts: Report of a formal investigation into ethnic minority recruitment*. London.

Council for National Academic Awards. 1984. *Supervised Work Experience in CNAA First Degree Courses: An appraisal*. CNAA Development Services Publication 5.

Craft, A and Craft, M. 1983. The participation of ethnic minorities in further and higher education. *Educational Research*, vol 21, no. 1.

Employment Gazette, January 1987. Ethnic origin and economic status. Department of Employment.

Employment Gazette, December 1988. Ethnic origin and the labour market. Department of Employment.

Field, J and Meadows, P. 1987. *National Survey of 1980 Graduates and Diplomates: Methodological report*. Social and Community Planning Research.

Gatley, D. 1988. The influence of social class origins on the choice of course, career preferences and entry to employment of CNAA graduates. PhD thesis, Staffordshire Polytechnic.

Gordon, A. 1981. The educational choices of young people. In *Access to Higher Education*, ed. O. Fulton. Society for Research into Higher Education. Guildford.

Grace, G. ed. 1984. *Education and the City*. London: Routledge and Kegan Paul.

Great Britain Central Statistical Office. 1988. *Social Trends*, no. 18. HMSO.

Gupta, Y. 1977. The educational and vocational aspirations of Asian immigrant and English school-leavers: A comparative study. *British Journal of Sociology*, vol 28, no. 2, pp 185–198.

Halsey, A, Heath, A F and Ridge, J. 1980. *Origins and Destinations: Family, class and education in modern Britain*. Oxford University Press.

Jenkins, R. 1986. *Racism and Recruitment: Managers, organisations and equal opportunity in the labour market*. Cambridge University Press.

Jenkins, R and Troyna, B. 1983. Educational myths, labour market realities. In *Racism, School and the Labour Market*, eds. B Troyna and D Smith. National Youth Bureau. Leicester.

Keenan, T. 1978. Interviewing for graduate recruitment. *Personnel Management*, vol 10, no. 2.

Kitwood, T and Borrell, C. 1980. The significance of schooling for an ethnic minority. *Oxford Review of Education*, vol 6, no. 3, pp 241–253.

Lyon, E. and Gatley, D. 1988. *Black Graduates and Labour Market Recruitment*. HELM working paper 7. Department of Social Sciences, Polytechnic of the South Bank.

McManus, I. and Richards, P. 1984. Audit of admissions to medical schools: I. acceptances and rejects, II. shortlisting and interviews, III. applicants' perceptions and proposals for change. *British Medical Journal*, vol 290, pp 319–320.

Rampton Committee. 1981. *West Indian Children in our Schools*. Cmnd 8273. London: HMSO.

Rand, T and Wexley, K. 1975. Demonstration of the effect 'similar to me' in simulated employment interviews. *Pyschological Report*, no. 36.

Roizen, J and Jepson, M. 1985. *Degrees for Jobs: Employer expectations of higher education*. SRHE and NFER. Nelson: Guildford.

Smith, D. 1977. *Racial Disadvantage in Britain*. London: Penguin.

Springbelt, B. 1958. Factors affecting the final decision in the employment interview. *Canadian Journal of Psychology*, vol 12, pp 13–22.

Swann Committee. 1985. *Education for All*. Cmnd. 9453. London: HMSO.

Tanna, K. 1985. Opening the black box. *Times Education Supplement*, 20 September, p 17.

Tanna, K. 1987. The experience of South Asian university students in the British educational system and in their search for work. PhD thesis, University of Aston.

Tavistock Institute of Race Relations. 1978. *Application of Race Relations Policy in the Civil Service*. London: HMSO.

Tomlinson, S. 1980. The educational performance of ethnic minority children. *New Community*, vol 8, no. 3, pp 213–234.

Tomlinson, S. 1984. *The Education of Ethnic Minority Children in Britain: A review of the literature*. London: Heinemann Educational Books.

Vellins, S. 1982. South Asian students at British universities: A statistical note. *New Community*, vol 10, no. 2, pp 206–212.

Verma, G. 1986. *Ethnicity and Educational Achievement in British Schools*. MacMillan.